Endorsements for
Beat the Wealth Management Hustle

"In *Beat the Wealth Management Hustle*, Andy points the way for you to determine who is working to make money for themselves, and who is working to make money for you. Having worked with Andy in the institutional investment industry for over thirty years, it is clear to me that he places his clients' interests ahead of his own. Sadly, this is rather rare. As Andy suggests, ask the hard questions, demand straightforward answers, and use these to evaluate your advisor's and their results. Beware those who obfuscate and bamboozle. Investing isn't overly complicated or hard. My rule is that if I can't understand what the advisor or investment manager is doing, I don't invest with them. Period."

–Mitchell Little, Managing Member
Coronado Investments LLC

"I had the honor of working for Andy at his investment advisory firm for several years. His unwavering commitment to daily diligence, thoughtful guidance, and genuine care for clients has left a lasting impression on me. Thanks to Andrew, I discovered my path to wise investment management, and I am confident that others reading his book will find the same clarity and gain the confidence they need. Andrew's insights empower readers to identify what truly matters when choosing an advisor – ensuring added value to their portfolios and not falling for the impressions of personalities and big names. As Andrew wisely points out, it is time for Wealth Management advisory services to undergo a transformative change."

–Asta Galinyte, Venture Partner at VU Venture Partners
and former colleague at Newport Capital Advisers LLC

"Andy's life experiences make him the ideal person to eliminate your investment anxiety. He outlines a disciplined and continuous structure for YOU to plan and implement an efficient investment program. Ask the right questions and become your own chief investment officer today. I could not more highly recommend reading this one as soon as possible!"
–Joel Salomon, Bestselling author of *Mindful Money Management, The 9 Money Rules Millionaires Use,* and *Infinite Love and Money*

BEAT THE
Wealth Management Hustle

BEAT THE
Wealth Management Hustle

Invest Independently to Grow Savings Faster
with Peace of Mind

ANDREW PARRILLO

Foreword by **Anthony Scaramucci**

Victory Road Advisors LLC

Published by Victory Road Advisors LLC

ISBN (paperback): 979-8-9898970-0-1
ISBN (ebook): 979-8-9898970-1-8

Book design and production by www.AuthorSuccess.com

Printed in the United States of America

Disclaimer:
This book is intended to provide general information about investing. It is not intended to offer investment advice and is not an offer to buy or sell or a solicitation of an offer to buy or sell any security or investment product or service. Information regarding investment services is provided solely to include information about my investment philosophy and framework for decision-making. This material is not to be construed as providing investment services in any jurisdiction where such offers or solicitation would be illegal. You should be aware that investments can fluctuate in price, value, and/or income, and you may get back less than you invested. Investments or investment services mentioned may not be suitable for you, and if you have any doubts, you should seek advice from your registered investment advisor. Presentation of the information is not intended to create, and receipt does not constitute a client relationship. Readers are advised not to act upon this information without seeking the service of a professional accountant, attorney, and/or registered investment advisor.

I dedicate this book to my parents, Marguerite Parrillo 1923-2017 and Carmine Parrillo who was born in 1924. My father to this day expresses optimism about the future and both parents taught me the values that were forged during some of the most challenging parts of our history in the past century.

December 13, 2023

CONTENTS

FOREWORD

AS AMERICANS, we live in the greatest country in the world. The opportunities we have to work hard and achieve our dreams, no matter where or what circumstances we come from, are unmatched. Throughout my career, I have been very fortunate to enjoy a measure of success, but the journey hasn't been a straight line and I have made more than my share of mistakes. Some of the mistakes have been small, and some of them have been big. That's what happens when you take risks. But the important thing when I make mistakes is that I acknowledge them, learn from them, and keep moving forward.

Andrew has always appreciated my willingness to admit mistakes and to learn from them. In the book, he discusses the importance of how investment managers, especially hedge fund managers, overcome and learn from disappointing performance intervals. It is axiomatic that all investors will face tests of their strategies. The key is to learn from our mistakes and resolutely adjust our processes. My path has always been deliberate, although randomness has sometimes interfered with my judgment and expectations. Like the author, my perspective has been to challenge conventional wisdom and remain independent with my decisions.

One of the most important lessons I have learned during my career is the importance of doing business with good people.

Whenever I am considering a possible business arrangement, I am focused much more on the character of the person on the other side of the table, rather than squeezing every basis point out of the partnership. I don't always make the right character judgments, but more times than not, doing business with the right people has proven to be the correct decision.

Of course, I have been vulnerable to some difficult and less-than-ideal outcomes, but I continue to learn from those mistakes. Each failure makes me a better entrepreneur. As an investor, it is essential to see things as they are, not what we may ideally like them to be. Our world has changed, and it is in our best interest to recognize changes even if they seem uncomfortable. Andrew's book is a wake-up call for all of us.

I believe that *Beat the Wealth Management Hustle* is important reading for all investors. The book advocates for the democratization of access for individual investors and a clear path to protect people from the longer-term deleterious side effects of inflation. It also urges transparency, and full disclosure by the investment management industry. Andrew challenges the legacy practices of the investment management industry and encourages everyday investors to embrace the opportunity to invest for the future, as well as disrupt a multi-trillion-dollar industry with a new and fairer fee model.

Another reason for supporting Andrew is that while people in finance and beyond know me, he is not well known, but his message is powerful and deserves attention. The power of the book is in its simplicity. Disclosure and transparency must be prioritized for individual investors.

Andrew Parrillo and I have been in the same industry, have shared similar experiences, interviewed the same investment managers, and have visited each other's offices over the past twenty years, but never met. We both allocated assets to investment managers for the benefit of our clients and we both marched to our own beat in a fragmented industry.

Technology and competition have improved individuals' access to high-quality investments, but the wealth management industry has maintained its legacy fee practices that have not necessarily benefited clients. One of my favorite quotes is from John Maynard Keynes: "When the facts change, I change my mind. What do you do, sir?" It is time for a change in the multi-trillion-dollar wealth management industry that will benefit investors. We have seen how disruption of major industries has lowered costs and has improved services and access in the past twenty years. Investing should be no different.

Anthony Scaramucci
November 2023

OVERVIEW AND SUMMARY

Lessons Learned from Decades as an Institutional Investor for All Investors

PERHAPS THE MOST ILLUMINATING question one could ask me is: What problems have I solved? The problems that I have solved for former clients and want to solve with this book are to reduce the anxiety that individuals may have about investing, to eliminate or greatly reduce their ongoing fees, and to produce optimal outcomes with their money.

The four critical questions that investors must answer are 1) How much investment risk do I want, 2) How much risk do I have in my portfolio, 3) How much risk do I need to optimize my prospects for achieving my goal, and 4) How much will investment expenses reduce my return?

My investment advisory experiences span decades working with individual and institutional investors through many financial market cycles and a few crashes. When markets were doing well there was little for me or other advisors to do, but we earned our keep when we helped clients establish their strategies and navigate difficult and what to many were frightening declines in stock and bond markets. I relate what worked for investors over those decades so what I discuss in this book is my reality, not some theoretical idea.

Opportunity for All

My intention is to simplify and demystify the investment process for beginning investors and to help experienced investors optimize their investment processes and their relationships with advisors they may engage. For those with advisors I detail questions to ask them to evaluate their effectiveness to add value after their fees. Advisory fees can be many thousands of dollars and investors should understand how much they may pay and what value they receive.

All those wishing to invest can do so with no minimum dollar requirements. One very well-known firm offers index funds with zero fees and no minimum investment. Access for all who want to save and have the best chance to preserve their money's buying power over time can do so. The biggest impediment to investment success is not to start. The major points of this book are that one must have a perspective on stock market behavior and calibrate their investments to align with their specific, prospective risk and return preferences, that fees and other investment expenses matter, and that compound interest is a much more powerful force than many may appreciate.

What about guarantees from insurance companies?

Wait a minute. Why should I assume the risk of loss with stock investing when I can get a guarantee from an insurance company? It is important to remember that insurance firms that offer a variety of guarantees do so for a profit, and they should plainly disclose their terms and total charges. Insurance has a cost that may be justified but must be understood along with the terms governing such contracts. In addition to understanding the benefits, those considering insurance policies should know exactly what the agent is paid in commissions and over what period, what the insurance company charges for benefits and administrative expenses, and what the termination charges or penalties may be. Insurance companies may offer seductive terms for saving with tax advantages and other comforting features for life insurance, annuities of various types that deliver future benefits, principal protection for investment in stock indices, interest-free access to loans from accumulated value, and long-term care policies. Risk management vehicles represented by insurance policies may be part of one's financial plan, but not necessarily an entire plan. (I discuss bank savings accounts in the chapter on investment choices, but they have not offered returns after inflation and taxes to match those of stock investing over time.)

Are you getting value from your advisor?

If investors with advisors are receiving returns after all fees and expenses above those of a stock market index, such as the S&P 500 benchmark, they are fortunate. Advisors should provide after-fee performance comparisons that mirror the client's asset allocation and usually include not just the S&P 500 but other relevant indices in proportion to their actual allocations. Why a benchmark such as the S&P 500 stock index? The S&P 500 Composite Stock Price Index is comprised of those domestically based corporations with publicly traded stock that meet the Standard & Poor's stock selection committee's criteria. Its historical performance has long been a benchmark for investors. It has been a broad measure of corporate performance for nearly one hundred years. During that long interval, the total annualized rate of return with dividends reinvested with no taxes charged was about 10%. The Index had several long and steep declines in those hundred years but has recovered the losses and advanced to new high levels. It is an index in which to invest that can cost very little or nothing. Why pay someone to try to match its return after their advisory fees?

If investors with advisors are not receiving measurable asset value increases after fees relative to a benchmark, they can accelerate their asset growth by saving fees and investing independently. Fee savings accrue quickly and are significant. Investors with a plan and clear expectations of portfolio behavior can better maintain the resolve to stay on a long-term strategy when the stock market declines significantly—and it will, just as it will recover in time if history is a guide. More things can happen than will happen, and we should prepare for the most likely outcomes. Armageddon and Nirvana are extremes that are unlikely to visit investors, although some may feel like they have and should resist emotional responses to stock market fluctuations. Stock markets have been very productive for investors who have remained resolute but have been unrewarding for those who have sold after stock market declines.

Beat the Wealth Management Hustle describes a framework for those who want to invest their assets efficiently with confidence and know what to expect from their portfolios for six months and longer. Investors should know what to expect before the stock market declines significantly.

In addition to helping investors evaluate their advisors and develop optimal relationships with them, this book outlines a disciplined and continuous structure for everyday people to plan and implement efficient investment programs independently. I share what I learned as an institutional investor to simplify the investment process and to take the anxiety out of investing, or at least reduce it to a probable level that we can accept.

What is wealth?

Is wealth just money and financial assets, or is it more? To me health is ultimate wealth, and so-called wealth managers do not necessarily contribute to my physical well-being. Wealth to me is also gratitude for one's health, family and friends, the freedom of choice, and the ability to contribute to the well-being of others. Financial wealth surely provides a potentially large measure of comfort regarding safe domicile, adequate food, educational opportunities, freedom on how one spends one's time, freedom to travel, and the ability to contribute time and money to eleemosynary initiatives. But none of those necessarily require a wealth manager. I have always considered the process of managing assets as investment management, and the term "wealth manager" is specious to me. It has become a convenient and aspirational term to promote investment management services.

Of course, some organizations assist those with significant financial assets to efficiently manage their assets including the best estate planning, business succession, tax strategies, retirement saving strategies, and risk management strategies including insurance, but most investors and so-called wealth managers are not in that realm. Most individual investors may benefit from the advice of a fixed-fee Certified Financial Planner (CFP) regarding the most efficient retirement vehicles, legacy planning, tax decisions, and risk management programs generally centered around insurance products. A CPA who takes a holistic approach to clients can also be a reliable source of financial planning advice and is typically the most trusted advisor for most individuals after their physician.

This book addresses investment management, not financial planning. Many people can benefit from discussing their finances with a planner or their CPA. This is especially true with business owners. The benefits of engaging a planner will probably only be evident after their rigorous and systematic review of a client's profile of assets, liabilities, income, retirement planning, legacy planning, and risk management, such as that which insurance can address. Of course, one's attorney should be consulted regarding estate planning, will, and potential benefits of trusts. Even those with modest assets and income can probably benefit from engaging a professional financial planner.

I review asset-based fee investment advisors, Internet-based advisory services, a do-it-yourself approach, and a consultative, investment planning approach focused on rigorous and objective goal determination, implementation, and reviews on a fixed fee basis. Of course, the one variable that is easily determined and managed is the fees paid for advice or management.

What investors can do

1. Engage a registered investment advisor for an asset-based annual fee.
2. Do-it-yourself and invest independently to save valuable fees and accumulate savings faster.
3. As a bridge between do-it-yourself and a full-time investment advisor, investors may want to engage a registered investment advisor to assist in formulating and implementing a strategy and provide on-demand advice after initial implementation for a fixed fee. Think of this option as an investment planner and coach.

Investing is not a mystery, and no one should be intimidated by the process. The focus of the book is on understanding the nature of financial assets in general, but more specifically what one can expect from the stock market and in that context, one's behavior influencing their investment decisions. There is every reason to expect that investors can invest independently, or with the assistance of advisors, with joy and peace of mind.

A path to fearless investing

- **The world has changed significantly in the past twenty years, but the wealth management industry has not.**
- Technology and competition have made investing exceptionally low or even at no cost for the necessary services and investment vehicles.
- The wealth management industry knows that it does not perform better than a broad index fund composite after its fees. If it did, it would be advertising that fact. If your advisor's return after fees and expenses is adding value over an index fund return, you have chosen wisely, and you would be in rare company.
- Many clients of wealth management firms do not know what and when they pay, or that they pay the advisor every day for as long as they retain them. The same clients do not know or even ask if the advisor has a competitive investment advantage.
- Most wealth management clients pay for comfort while the advisors get paid to take risks with client assets. That sounds backward but it is true.
- Asset management fees are based on a percentage of assets under management annually, so fees are accrued daily. Does your advisor work on your account every business day?
- A fixed fee approach to determine risk and reward on a short and long-term basis, investment implementation, and documented investment policy serve the client by minimizing fees while offering access to ongoing institutionally informed and professional investment coaching.

- Fees matter much more than most think and are the one element that investors can control. Securities regulations stipulate that investment management fees are negotiable. Has your advisor told you that fact?
- Investing is not a mystery and need not be intimidating to the everyday investor. Stock investing is only for those who understand the risks and have a sufficiently long investment horizon, usually ten years or more.
- This book is about efficient investing, not financial planning. Investors should engage appropriate professionals for help with tax planning and compliance, estate planning, retirement planning, risk management (insurance), and business succession or sale advice, to name the more important items.

EDUCATE AND CLARIFY

Your Best Interests: Knowledge is Power

WHAT PROMPTED ME TO WRITE THIS BOOK? In December 2022 I was invited to join a friend at her community charity group's holiday party. We entered a large house in the country on a brisk night with about forty guests. The party was well underway when we arrived, and the conversation was vibrant. I did not know anybody at the party. The first person I met was the host and it happens that he and I had the same passion for food and cooking, so we shared our recipe preferences and favorite cookbooks. We also talked about our dogs. A good and welcoming start. Others I met wanted to know about me, which was also welcoming and in the spirit of the season. I told them I that have three sons and three grandchildren and that I had retired from the investment advisory business a few years earlier.

Several people then asked me what they should do with their investments because they were concerned about the nearly 20% decline in stock prices and 15% in bond prices in 2022. I told them that I no longer offered investment advice but gently suggested that they should ask their advisors. I was quite surprised that they asked someone that they did not know for investment advice. The subject of money and investments requires context and confidentiality and does not lend itself to quick answers, so I tend to avoid discussing such personal topics casually. I did not ask them why they had not asked their advisors, or had they done so, why they did not share the answer. Had they shared their advisor's comments, I would have deferred to opine, as I would not want to create any doubt the individual may have had about the advisor. It was clear to me that they should have been better informed about the subject and specifically about their accounts by their respective advisors, without having to ask a stranger.

All I wanted to do at the party was learn about the group's community work, especially its food bank and homeless programs, and maybe talk about sports, but the investment questions continued as we managed our buffet plates. They asked me what I thought the Federal Reserve Bank (Fed) would do with its interest rate policy the next week when it had its meeting to determine and then announce its next policy steps, or guidance. For context, the Fed had begun raising interest rates at an aggressive pace starting nine months earlier in March 2022, and its various members had made regular statements that the Fed would continue to raise interest rates until price inflation began to subside. The questions about the Fed's pending announcement the following week revealed that party guests were focused on financial market news, but in my view, they did not have the context necessary to gauge the implications of Fed policy. It clearly and understandably confused them, along with probably millions of others. I allowed that my expectation was that the Fed would continue with the same policy course that its members had telegraphed weekly to the media for months, but my guess was that a shift in policy that might influence short-term investment decisions was unlikely. I thought that I could help them learn more about context by suggesting that they pose their questions to their advisors.

The fact that the people did not talk with their advisors about their current concerns about the market decline and Fed policy and its implications was my epiphany and the beginning of my journey to write this book. I had been encouraged to write a book for several years by those with whom I talked regularly after retirement but did not have a message until the holiday party conversations. At that point, my mind was flooded with ideas about a book drawn from my career working with people through some of the most challenging stock market periods in our lifetimes.

In the next few months, several other people whom I know also asked me about the stock market. Again, I declined to offer advice, but because I knew them, I began asking a few more questions about their relationship with their advisors. The questions are detailed in the chapter entitled "Eliminate Investment Anxiety," but briefly: 1) How much and when do they pay advisory fees? 2) Do they receive regular, clear investment performance reports with their rate of return after fees with a comparison to returns from a composite of market indices in which one could invest for little or no cost? 3) What are their advisor's structural advantages to add value to their account? 4) How their advisors determine their specific risk and return preferences? And 5) If they have an investment policy statement that their advisor reviews with them at least annually? None had ready answers to these basic due diligence questions. My message and mission became quite clear after my "aha" moment. It was time for me to offer my perspective with this book. My goal is to motivate investors to embrace the investment process optimally starting with fundamental questions, and to do so with joy and peace of mind and not be intimidated by the subject.

It is important to note that some of the investors I talked with expressed satisfaction with their advisors and although they did not know objectively if their advisors added value to their portfolios, they were comfortable with the arrangement. I cannot define "comfort" exactly but those with advisors can probably relate to the notion. Of course, they had confidence in their advisors, but they did not understand what they were paying their advisors for beyond a sense of relative comfort. Nor did they appreciate that if they allowed inertia to keep them from asking their advisors penetrating questions and just maintain the status quo, they would pay the advisor daily for the rest of their lives without knowing what economic value they received.

What is the wealth management hustle? It refers to those managers who do not deliver measurable value to their clients after their fees, and not just a presumably informed perspective on the investment landscape and comforting dialogue after a financial market decline, but do not deliver measurable value to their clients. They should also provide objectively determined client risk and return parameters when establishing investment goals within the client's respective time horizon. If your investment manager consistently performs better than a market benchmark that mirrors the allocations in your portfolio comprised of market indices, or composed index benchmarks, you have chosen your manager wisely. Your advisor should deliver periodic reports, usually quarterly, of your portfolio performance after their fees compared to your composed index benchmark. Unfortunately, many engage investment managers who do not produce rates of return after their fees that exceed a composite of market indices. Clients must hold their advisors accountable for the fees that they charge.

The chapter entitled "Eliminate Investment Anxiety," reviews in more detail the questions that investors should ask their investment managers. If they do not ask these questions they may be unduly influenced by the firm's size, aspirational advertising, the engaging and persuasive personalities of the advisor(s), and/or the recommendation of friends. It is not a stretch to say that many are intimidated by the investment process and its challenges, and so they defer to investment managers for ongoing advice.

Investment manager fees typically are annual and are based on the asset value that accrues daily, whether the advisor performs daily functions or not. One reason that clients may not immediately recall their management fees is that they have authorized their advisors to charge their custodial accounts for fees. Clients do not have to pay each quarterly fee with a separate authorization or payment. They should request separate notices every time a fee is charged to their account. Many of us get immediate notices of charges to our credit cards on our mobile devices, so why not an alert about their advisor's fees? I believe that many if not most clients are captive to their advisors because of inertia and the reluctance to examine if they are receiving value.

As an aside, it is a regulatory requirement that all advisory fees be negotiable. Has your advisor informed you of this requirement? The established investment managers may find it uncomfortable to answer these perhaps stubborn questions, but it is in the best interest of individual investors to understand the answers.

My goal is to serve what is in the investor's best interest, especially when investors are terrified that they will lose even more value after a significant market decline and believe that their best interest is to cut and run.

There is little question that investing can be challenging for everyone, including professionals. It is not possible to measure uncertainty, but it is possible to measure investment risk based on the history of financial behavior. If we establish rules and habits about our investment process, we can optimize risk and our reaction to the inevitable unexpected outcomes that financial market randomness can produce. It is essential for our opportunity and risk management to document a framework for our decisions. This requires an appreciation of financial market history, both current and distant, and can be measured mathematically. Financial markets reflect human reactions to numerous variables as investors assess the future returns on their assets. We can measure human reactions to factors that impact asset values and use probability analysis to structure our investment strategy and portfolio holdings. This approach is broadly known as behavioral finance and its research can guide us. Daniel Kahneman is a psychologist and won the Nobel Prize in Economic Sciences in 2002. His book *Thinking Fast and Slow,* published by Farrar, Straus and Giroux, 2011, reviews the benefits of careful consideration to avoid emotional responses to gains and losses. This theory is put into practical action with his Prospect Theory, explained in a later chapter, and helps people to explore their preferences for value increases or declines that they may express in their investment choices. This process is the basis of my firm's approach to risk and reward assessment. There are no immutable rules in behavioral finance, but over time patterns of behavior can be measured and used to help us understand the probable course of our investment program and our portfolio values.

I highlight what should be clear about the wealth management hustle, pitch, or scheme and offer a commonsense approach for individual investors to get what they pay for in dollars and cents. Those dollars and cents paid to investment managers are potentially very significant even in the short term but are amplified in the long term. The word "hustle" can connote hard work, determination, and resourcefulness, or it can mean a lack of transparency and authenticity. Characterizing the so-called wealth management industry as a hustle is not necessarily a pejorative reference, but it is when it denotes pretense which sadly is too often the case.

I believe that many people have been persuaded about the difficulty of understanding the investment process and have not been educated about it, or the alternatives, to paying ongoing daily fees, often for a lifetime. This perspective is reinforced by ubiquitous advertising to convince us of our *pain points* when it comes to making decisions about our money in an uncertain world. The so-called wealth management industry has expertly capitalized, or more accurately exploited the uncertainty that investors may have about investing independently and extract fees from client assets that accrue daily.

Pain points? Sure, if one wants to despair, or be sad or fearful about investing, there are always the big or small sophisticated firms at the ready to deliver comfort to the investor. I look at the process differently. Before I go any further, let me reinforce that if we have decided to invest for the future, we should embrace the freedom to do so with joy and peace of mind. If not joy and peace of mind about our investments, what is the alternative? Should we worry, be anxious or have other negative emotions that may surround our relationship with money and look to others for comfort? ***Invest with purpose, clarity, information, and carefully derived expectations.*** If I can deliver reasons for a confident, anxiety-free, and even fearless approach to investing, I will have accomplished my mission.

There is one other important message that requires reinforcement and that is the power of compounding fee savings, which is often regarded as a trivial aspect of investing but is not, as is illustrated below with examples of the significant compounded dollar cost of fees.

Most people do not wake up each morning thinking about making important or difficult decisions about their investments because, it is easier for them to leave those decisions to an advisor who is compensated for the risk born by the client. That sentiment is understandable because the media reports what may be confusing and seemingly chaotic news about financial markets, and investors may have had negative outcomes when they have tried to invest in stocks independently. If such investors are pleased with the advisory arrangement without an objective measure of the value that their advisors have added after the fees charged, this book should change their perspective.

I am not averse to investment advisory services if they add value after their fees. Let us look at what many believe is a trivial number of 1%, which is approximately the annual fee that most advisors charge. For perspective, one can construct a portfolio that captures significant, diversified opportunities for fees of about one-tenth of 1%, or even zero, with no minimum investment amount. Let us further assume that a 7% annual rate of return is reasonable for the purpose of illustration and a typical goal of long-term investors in tax-free retirement accounts. If one invests $500,000 now and earns 7% annually for twenty years, the ending value would be $1,934,842. The value at a 6% annual rate of return, which is what you would earn after paying the annual 1% to your advisor would be $1,603,568. If you think that your advisor delivers $331,274 in value over twenty years, then that is your decision. What if you paid yourself the $331,274? That is what you would get if you did not pay 1% advisory fees and generated a 7% annual rate of return. If twenty years seems too long, then let us compare the values after ten years at 7% and 6% annualized rates of return. At 7% the value after ten years would be $983,576, and at 6% the value would be

$895,424. You may want to pay yourself the $88,152 difference. It would be wonderful if your advisor could generate more than 7% a year after fees. Extracting a premium of even 1% or 2% after fees over the stock market return is not necessarily easy. If your advisor can produce excess net of fee returns consistently you should be very pleased with their services. If not, then take action to save fees and produce returns that a low or no cost index fund will generate.

In addition to helping investors evaluate their advisors and develop optimal relationships with them, I will outline a disciplined and continual structure for everyday people to plan and implement efficient investment programs independently. I encourage investors to simplify the investment process and reduce or eliminate any anxiety of investing. I will describe my approach to efficient opportunity and risk management based on the process that we used resolutely and successfully for twenty-five years advising my own former firm's endowment, pension, and high-net-worth clients. As a step between engaging an asset-based fee advisor and a do-it-yourself approach, I have initiated an advisory service that is a fixed-fee, low-cost alternative for all investors. It provides customized consultation, disciplined investment objective determination, and on-demand check-ins. Aside from initial planning and strategy formulation, one can consider the process as a second opinion to determine if implied portfolio risk is aligned with the client's risk and opportunity preferences.

You can take charge of your financial future with an investment decision process used by institutional investors. Individual investors, or "retail investors" as the regulators describe non-institutional investors, have easy access, low-cost and efficient investment vehicles. I advocate that individual investors invest at wholesale or zero costs, not retail prices. Access to low-cost vehicles and services has been available for approximately the past ten years, which can be characterized as democratizing investment. Democratizing means that everyone has access to prudent investment vehicles. The head of the largest mutual fund and advisory firm recently said in an interview that his firm is democratizing investing. Other major firms agree that democratizing the process is in the best interest of the investor, although the majority promote legacy services because the profit margins of such recurring revenue businesses are quite attractive. Indeed, a review of those publicly traded investment firms' quarterly filings with the Securities and Exchange Commission (SEC) reveal the importance of investment advisory services to those firms and in the footnotes, the average fees as a percentage of their assets under management.

The evolution of the investment industry has changed more quickly than some, or even many, are aware of, but the investment management industry has maintained its legacy asset-based pricing model to the likely detriment of most investors. Professionals cling to the notion that they can persuade the public that the individual does not have the interest, ability, confidence, or time to manage their own investment programs, and they have been successful in promoting this narrative. The message of established brokerages, mutual funds, and advisory firms is reinforced by advertising that is clearly aspirational, and not definitive about the advice for which those firms charge fees or the value that they add. The regulators may want to consider requiring advisors to disclose the cumulative cost of their services over several time horizons to those apocryphal customers in the advertisements. This would not be dissimilar to the regulatory requirement that mutual funds disclose such information in their prospectuses. All those reasons are why I can characterize the wealth management business as a hustle.

You may rightly ask why I question investment management fees that are based on a legacy model of charging a percentage of asset market value annually, since I benefited from asset-based fees for my entire career. The answer is two-fold. First, my firm reported performance after our fees at least quarterly and always compared those results to a relevant composite of stock and bond market unmanaged indices, in which the client could invest on their own with no or very low fees through Exchange Traded Funds (ETFs) on their own. Our clients, mostly fiduciaries themselves, not independent investors, always knew how their portfolios performed and could objectively evaluate our added value. The second is that we charged relatively low fees for our non-discretionary services for our consultative clients. Although we did not direct clients' investments in consultative relationships, our clients almost always accepted our recommendations for changes in allocations. They received regular performance reports that compared their returns to their objectives, relevant market indices, and peer funds.

How did we add value over index returns after fees? As I will explain, our approach was creative for marginal allocations that often generated handsome incremental rates of return, because we stayed off the well-worn path of other institutional investors. Briefly, we were early adopters of newer mutual funds, hedge funds, and investment advisory strategies that most institutional investment firms avoided because of career risk and or because the assets that they managed were too large for smaller funds or capacity-limited strategies. My experience led me to this book and new model advisory service because I believe that it is in the best interest of investors. The other vital point is the need to simplify the process to capture returns offered by broad stock indices and save fees. This approach is not for casual social conversation because it is not exciting, but it is a probable path to preserve purchasing power in the long term.

The career risk is that an unconventional decision that has a negative outcome subjects the individual to undesirable employment or reputational consequences. As John Maynard Keynes, the British economist said, "Worldly wisdom teaches that it is better for reputation to fail conventionally than to succeed unconventionally." It is common in the institutional investment industry for advisors to favor larger, established firms to which they allocate assets, just as it is common for mutual fund managers to maintain individual security positions that will track the benchmark index, often the S&P 500 Composite Stock Price Index, so as not to deviate too much from the index performance. These are examples of how to avoid career risk.

Highlighted topics

- Invest with purpose, clarity, information, carefully derived expectations, and with joy, not fear.
- You are your own chief investment officer, even if you engage a professional advisor.
- The importance of your investment policy and adherence to its strategy.
- The importance of determining your investment risk tolerance before it is exceeded.
- Why you should invest with the risk of loss to preserve your purchasing power into the future.
- Understand what, when, and why you are paying your investment advisor. Fees matter.
- Any question about your money is a fair question.
- Definitions of service providers and investment vehicles.

- Stock investing offers the highest probability of maintaining the purchasing power of your money in liquid assets despite its volatility.
- Embrace the opportunity and engage the no-cost services of brokerage firms and mutual funds.
- What is risk?
- Due diligence checklist for investors to evaluate their advisors.

WHAT ARE MY CORE VALUES?

I AM ALWAYS IMPRESSED by those individuals and businesses that express their values, so here are mine: My guiding values include kindness, humility, transparency, common sense, passion, clarity, and a basic understanding of why anyone would own common stock. In full transparency, I discuss my solution to an advisory problem that describes my new model or I believe, new era advisory firm that has the potential to disrupt the multi-trillion-dollar, entrenched wealth management industry. It offers a cost-efficient method for those who prefer professional coaching about their investment strategy but do not want to pay fees daily for an indefinite period.

I started Newport Capital Advisers, my SEC registered firm, in 1995 as an institutional investment advisory consulting firm, in a very competitive sector, with many large and well-established firms. I was fortunate to receive unsolicited referrals to prospective endowment, pension, family investment offices, and high-net-worth individual clients. When prospective clients asked for my presentation, I started by telling them that they did not need my services because they could very probably produce at least average performance relative to funds with similar objectives by just allocating to an S&P 500 Index fund and a bond fund in a conventional percentage allocation for their respective peer group. I also illustrated the value of modest incremental returns if the investor was open to less conventional allocations. I guess I never got the memo that investment advisors should always push hard for a sale. The simple reason for this is that they would save on investment management fees, and in any event, most mutual funds or separately managed portfolios rarely beat the S&P 500's performance with consistency after all the fees. That was in 1995 and is as true today as it was then, although today the expense of investing in the S&P 500 Composite Stock Index is much less. One popular vehicle that invests in the S&P 500 charges a total of three one-hundredths of one percent, or 0.03%. For perspective, one of the largest and oldest brokerage firms sponsored an unmanaged S&P 500 Stock Index mutual fund that charged an annual fee on the asset value of 0.65%. This allocation was in one of our college endowment client's portfolios in the late 1990s, and the first change recommendation that we made to that client was to invest in a lower-expense S&P 500 Index fund.

Adding value above the net returns of indexed portfolios required a more creative approach to distinguish my firm, as discussed in the next chapter. My simple solution was to add promising strategies, usually managed by newer and smaller firms than those on the well-worn institutional path. Firms that we focused on typically addressed the less efficient financial market verticals and demonstrated acumen in extracting a premium over their respective sector benchmark indices. Moreover, the smaller firms did not require the liquidity of the very large firms and strategies, so they could exploit opportunities much more easily. The most promising strategies and firms that we identified either did not have long performance records or enough assets under their management to which larger funds could allocate sufficient assets. Institutional investors generally do not want to have a disproportionate share of a management firm's assets. This distinction created an opportunity for my firm to allocate modest sums to smaller, talented investment managers.

I often referred to our manager selection strategy as a talent arbi-trage, for the simple reason that liquidity constraints inhibited large institutional investors from allocating to such firms.

Importantly, we were open to reviewing all strategies and did not arbitrarily exclude unknown firms from our universe. We were solicited by numerous investment firms globally and were always clear to them about our client objectives and our selection criteria. We always respected the commitment that these investment man-agement firms made to excellence in a very competitive and often unforgiving environment for strategies of all types from angel-stage venture capital to unhedged large capitalized publicly traded stocks.

One of the benefits of our position was the ability to learn from many of the most talented people in the investment community. This strategy was especially productive because many of the firms that we believed were promising delivered for our clients and grew, occasionally to the size that prompted us to release the firm. We were known for being open and not dogmatic with our initial criteria in reviewing potential firms. We were also candid with prospective investment firms about how we viewed their com-petitive position, which was a perspective that they appreciated. This led to referrals from those who appreciated our more open approach than most of the larger consulting firms, which we were told did not even grant interviews to many of our best newer man-agers, because they were too small or did not have a long record of performance or large client list. In the past, the quip that people used to describe the phenomenon of favoring large established investment firms was, "Nobody ever got fired for buying IBM." We all now know that other information technology firms have offered very competitive products and services, and their obvious success speaks to their effectiveness, even though they started as small firms. Our best information technology investment manager started in the 1970s and stayed with what became a very unpopular sector after the disc-drive-driven stock decline that began in mid-1983 and lasted through 1990. He was involved in initialing funding people who became giants in today's information technology companies and operated in a sector with little or no competition. The sector was small to micro-capitalized information technology companies, value-driven turnaround situations, which proved to be quite profitable and popular after 1991. Value-driven refers to investments in companies that often have modest growth prospects and underutilized assets.

Those who seek comfort in their investment decisions most often find it with the very largest firms. Are such firms large because they have the best advertising and marketing programs, or because their investment results and client service are superior to other firms? You will have to ask yourself and your prospective advisor the same questions.

HOW DID I GET HERE AND
WHAT DOES IT MEAN TO YOU?

BEFORE DESCRIBING MY PATH as an institutional investment advisor, I want to share a conversation I had with one of my three sons after I started my own firm. He asked what I did, and I told him that I advised investors, primarily fiduciaries on governing boards of endowment funds and family investment offices on how to invest their program's assets. His response was: "Hey Dad, that must take guts," although he did not use the word "guts."

I explained to him that I embraced it as a responsibility and challenge, and it never occurred to me that I might be viewed as having "guts" to advise others about investing their money. To me, it required discipline and adherence to simple principles, not leaps of faith or courage. Not unlike the fact that earlier in my life as an Air Force navigator I never thought about the prospect of crashing and burning, but instead just focused on performing my duties.

I began my investment career in the early 1970s after my active-duty military service, and at age thirty-two in 1979 was managing the retirement investment department of the largest bank in Rhode Island, which eventually became part of the Bank of America. Purely coincidentally, I started the month that the U.S. left the gold standard in August 1971, about which we dive deeper later in the book. The broad stock market averages, despite multiple market declines, have produced approximately a 10% a year total return since that time as the purchasing power of the dollar declined by about 87%. After the bank, I worked at a couple of independent firms in the Boston area.

After graduating from Boston University in May 1969 I entered a training program at the second-largest bank in Rhode Island, my home state, and joined the Air National Guard to fulfill my military obligation at the urging of my parents. It was a decision that was not my first choice, as I was ready to serve voluntarily on active duty. They were insistent because my father was a World War II veteran from the European theater and did not want me to experience the inevitable horrors of war, then in Vietnam. The Air National Guard was unlikely to be in combat at that point so was considered safe. It was my first real test in independent thinking, and I failed. I never again failed to make independent decisions about my life—or investments. Once on active duty for training, I petitioned the Air National Guard to join the active-duty Air Force, but it denied my request.

The first stop in the bank training program was a commercial bank credit department of a national bank. I spent a few months there and then I was off to flight training as an Air Force navigator for a year. After flight school, I re-entered the bank training program and was directed to the retirement investment department of the largest trust department in the state. As odd as it may seem now, the investment industry was not the favored career path of many recent college graduates. One reason perhaps is that the focus on measuring investment performance was increasing in the retirement plan industry, so accountability was quite clear and based on pure math. A few years later Congress enacted the Employee Retirement Income Security Act (ERISA) that focused attention on prudent governance of retirement assets. I favored a competitive environment so reporting investment performance to bank clients was an attractive challenge to me. It happened that my portfolios were populated by what was termed the "Nifty Fifty," which were stocks of large faster-growing companies that performed well when I was at that bank into 1973, compared to the market indices.

Very little was automated at the time and performance measurement required manual input of data onto paper tape. At that point, the typical reports to personal and even retirement trust clients consisted of meeting occasionally and reviewing the portfolio and objectives in a quiet conference room at the bank, or at the bank dining room, but rarely was performance reporting a central point of discussion. Also, the primary measure or benchmark of stock market performance was the level of the Dow Jones Industrial Average and did not include the broader and more representative Standard and Poor's Composite Stock Price Index. If one checks the fifth to the last page of the *Wall Street Journal* in the early 1970s, one will find a very short list of mutual funds. The second and third to last page had all the listings of New York Stock Exchange listed securities, and the fourth to last had listings for the American Stock Exchange. Financial markets and investment vehicles have advanced and expanded at an extraordinary pace since then. I was fortunate to have a mentor at the bank who was the well-respected, long-time head of investment research. He obviously saw something in me that I did not at that time. I did not have an MBA from a prestigious college, nor did I come from a wealthy family, which often characterized those who were offered prime positions in trust departments at that or any bank at the time. I had never owned a stock. Yes, it was a different era. I served in the Air National Guard for eleven years as a senior navigator and resigned at age thirty-three to spend more time with my family and to devote what, at that point, was a new and demanding position as the head of the retirement trust and investment division.

After positions at a Boston independent advisory firm and then an institutional consulting firm, I left to form my own firm. I had never been a broker, nor had I been compensated by brokerage commissions; and the firms that I had been at relied on asset-based fees as well brokerage commissions without full and transparent disclosure to clients, which at the time was accepted by the regulators. I did not agree with the policies of the consulting firms, because they did not disclose the commissions they received from the firms for trading in their client accounts by managers that the consulting firm recommended, so I struck out on my own where I controlled the ethics and policies. The pay-to-play approach of consulting firms at the time was not necessarily in the client's best interest despite being nominally in compliance with regulations. Why pay-to-play? Because the management firms could direct brokerage commissions to the consulting firms that recommended them—and usually did so. The SEC addressed and corrected this clear potential conflict of interest several years after I left to form my own firm.

In 1995, I founded my own, independent SEC-registered fee-only investment advisory firm and, as mentioned enjoyed unsolicited client relationships with endowment funds, pension funds, and family investment offices. Fee-only meant that I did not solicit or accept sales commissions of any kind. Clients of the former firm respected my independent thinking and fee approach. My primary activity was capital market and investment management firm research, to gauge to which firms I should allocate client assets, as well as establishing investment strategy and policy, inducing asset allocation and portfolio implementation. I also began offering discretionary services as an indelible statement of confidence in my process.

As a former portfolio manager at other firms, I believe that I was uniquely qualified to evaluate investment managers, and they respected my perspective. Most consultants had never actually managed money for which they had to account with regular performance reports, yet they had enormous power to influence their clients about the funds in which their clients should invest. It is easy to understand why most consultants recommended those firms that were the largest and had the best recent investment performance records. After all, how could volunteer fiduciaries at governing boards of client funds object to hiring the "best" investment managers and their firms? Because I could relate to the challenges of managing stocks and bonds, and the processes that they executed, I earned the respect of the investment management industry and thus received client referrals from managers. My due diligence was guided by a rigorous framework and extensive checklist of factors, but its basic principles were that investment managers should be humble and passionate about their strategy, explain it simply, experience an interval of disappointing performance, learn from it, and be accessible and transparent. Of course, if they could not demonstrate the ability to add relative value structurally and persistently above typical benchmarks and time horizons, they were disqualified. My services were available on both a discretionary and consultative basis for nearly twenty-five years until I tried retirement at the end of 2019.

How did I distinguish my firm from others that were far larger and well known? Certainly not by following the same path as the big competitors with research and investment recommendations. I had to make a meaningful difference in performance within the bounds of prudence at the total portfolio level. I did this by allocating small positions to strategies and investment management firms, generally known as emerging managers, which managed what I believed to have asymmetrical risk prospects that exploited inefficient financial market verticals. A vertical may be an industry sector or security sector, such as convertible bonds or small and micro-capitalized stocks, for example. A micro-capitalized stock is one with a market capitalization of all its shares under one billion dollars. The definition has changed with the growth of the stock market, and in the 1990's microcap stocks were generally under five hundred million in capitalization. Fortunately for me, such strategies were usually in sectors of the market that were avoided by the large funds, due to relatively constrained capacity to accept large allocations while preserving investment flexibility. The managers that I identified tended to address strategies often too innovative, new, or small for the larger consulting firms to recommend to their clients.

How did an average person from Rhode Island persuade independent, sophisticated trustees to engage my advice when they could have engaged the largest, most established, and popular consulting firms? Although there are several such stories that I can describe, perhaps the most important was one with my largest endowment client, a mid-sized endowment fund (several hundred million dollars in value in 1995) with a long-serving investment committee comprised of heads of major corporations, private investors, and others in the community who supported the school. I was assigned to that client by my former firm, and it became my third unsolicited client when I started my own firm. The endowment fund in the mid-1990s had no exposure to small-capitalized stocks or information technology (IT) companies. IT companies had been in a bear market since mid-1983 when the disc drive mania gave way to major declines in the broader IT sector. Just ten years later there were many IT investment managers and funds, but in 1990 most investment managers had pivoted to the value style of stock investing, and only a half-dozen IT-focused managers were operating nationally. By 2000 many firms managed IT stock strategies. The stock market can be fairly characterized as one driven by trends or fashions.

In August 1990, my written report and recommendation to the committee was to add a small-capitalized manager focusing on IT. The committee rejected the recommendation at its late August 1990 meeting. You may recall that, at the time, the U.S. had initiated Desert Shield, and the S&P 500 was down 12.5% in the quarter that ended September 30, 1990, so the mood of the committee was not constructive on the stock market. I reiterated my recommendation in my early November third quarter 1990 report and letter, and when the committee met in November, one of the most influential and undoubtedly wealthiest members of the committee who missed the August meeting was present and asked why his colleagues rejected my recommendation. The committee immediately agreed and decided to interview my recommended investment manager in a special meeting in mid-January 1991. (It was always interesting to observe the dynamics of committee decison-making, as they frequently changed depending on who was present and the mood of the financial market.)

The manager I recommended focused on small capitalized, value-oriented, turnaround IT companies and had only about $50 million under management, so it was a small firm with only two investment professionals. The night before the meeting, the U.S. released a video of a guided missile that had targeted a chimney in Baghdad that started Desert Storm, perhaps highlighting the power of IT. The meeting was very interesting as the manager displayed two disc drives, which today seem ancient. One was about 4" x 8" x 2" and the newer one was about 3" x 4" x 0.75," or roughly half the size of the older one. He explained that Gordon Moore, the founder of Intel, whom he knew from his research visits to Silicon Valley, in 1965 posited that roughly every two years the number of transistors on microchips will double. This became known as Moore's Law. Of course, it is obvious now that computational capacity has become exponentially faster and more efficient. By the end of the meeting, the committee was quite enthusiastic and engaged the manager in late January 1991, who went on to generate 20% net annual rates of return for ten years for the endowment.

Coincidentally, one of the largest and most innovative multi-billion-dollar endowment funds engaged that manager the same month. It happens that its chief investment officer advocated not just funding creative and smaller investment management firms but also supporting them when they encountered negative performance intervals. My approach to investment managers after the engagement was to be supportive and focused on the consistency of their respective processes, as most strategies encounter difficult competitive intervals, but if consistent recover from them.

The supportive committee member's endorsement was a game-changer for me, and the endowment fund engaged me when I founded my own firm in the spring of 1995. He also supported several other unconventional recommendations to the benefit of the fund. A couple of years after I founded my firm, he hired it to advise his family assets which placed them comfortably in the ultra-high-worth category. One of the most gratifying moments in my entire career was when after one of the family's quarterly meetings in New York City, he pulled me aside and thanked me for everything that I had done to that point keeping the family on course with their investment strategy. Confidentiality prohibits me from discussing this happy phenomenon in more detail, but this individual was influential and incredibly supportive. I attribute his support to my independent thinking and resolve to provide what was in my client's best interests even if it was unconventional. One might imagine that the individual was solicited by the biggest investment and brokerage firms in the country, so he had an informed perspective.

I always served in a fiduciary capacity during my investment career and never as a commission-based broker representative. From day one in my own firm, I only charged fully transparent fees based on a relatively small percentage of assets under advisement and never sought or accepted one cent of securities commissions or mutual fund payments, nor did I ever pay one cent of referral fees. As a related initiative that drew on my firm's research into and recommendation to consulting clients of hedge funds, in 2000 I formed a limited partnership that invested in specialized hedge funds for twenty years until I decided to retire in early 2020 when I also closed my advisory firm. The fund was designed to deliver a stream of less-correlated, equity-like returns for those with unhedged public or private equity allocations, and it only received incentive compensation after the limited partners earned 10% a year after the annual management fee of 1%. Such hurdle rates are desirable, but not as common as they should be. Aside from identifying smaller firms our other structural advantage was simply a consistent adherence to a continuous and diligent review process and clear long-term strategy.

The focus on what generally has been known as emerging managers, usually newer, smaller firms is atypical in the institutional investment industry, where the investment officers and governing boards could avoid the risk of relative underperformance with index allocations, or portfolios that essentially tracked the index. It has been said that one cannot eat relative performance. This typically is invoked when stock markets have declined, sometimes for long periods. Relative performance is distinct from "absolute performance," which has become the industry vernacular for strategies that do not have declines in value or "drawdowns." Naturally, all performance is absolute, so I mention this because the industry has adopted seemingly odd terms to distinguish the two types of strategies. The fact is that in the post-World War II world, above-average relative performance, or even average relative performance, in the rising stock market environment has prevailed and has been quite productive if subject to periodic and even protracted declines. Absolute performance became a buzzword after the Dot Com Crash in 2000 and spawned numerous hedge funds and mutual funds that adopted strategies intended to produce positive returns when the stock market declined. They zigged when the stock market zagged, or at least that was the intention. Investors were attracted to such strategies because of their fear of another 50% plus stock market decline. Most such funds were more focused on not losing money than making money and consequently rarely performed better than a simple portfolio comprised of short to intermediate-term U.S. Treasury securities. Recall that interest rates began their decline from 16%+ U.S. Treasury bond yields in 1981 to below one percent yields by 2020, producing the longest bull market in bond prices in history. There is no free lunch. For more on this, read the chapter on Investment Choices.

Summary

- The author's history and perspective.
- The value of independent thinking and action.

RETIREMENT IS NOT FOR ME AND WHAT I AM DOING ABOUT IT

BEN FRANKLIN SAID, "We do not stop playing when we grow old. We grow old when we stop playing." Careful of what you wish for if it is the freedom of retirement. Retirement was not satisfying for me after closing my firm. Sure, I can keep busy with various activities, but applying my skills and experience to benefit others with an informed perspective offers me the opportunity to be challenged and energized. My first step in that direction is this book and the next my new era firm. Many people have expressed wonder to me how they ever had time to pursue their careers when they have so many things to keep them busy in retirement. Alas, I am not one of them.

The idea of being free of any obligations with the ability to travel, pursue hobbies that we may not have time for during our careers, and/or devote more time to our families, and to charities, seems sweet and is a conventional view of retirement. My decision after three years of trying the conventional approach to retirement was to continue doing what energized me for most of my adult life, and that is staying involved with helping others in the investment process. This time I will do it on a more efficient scale, but no less important one than when I ran my firm for more than two decades. I am competitive and enjoy the challenge of investing. I also want to draw attention to the conventional asset-based fee model, that nearly all approximately15,000 registered investment advisors use, which is not necessarily in the best interest of clients. I believe that unless there is incontrovertible evidence of persistent value added, it overcharges, and in many cases has not reduced fees over the years.

I took time to reflect on how I could stay engaged in the industry that energized my career and concluded recently that I can add value in two ways: expressing the lessons that I learned in my career working with institutional and wealthy individual investors in this book to empower everyday investors with information, and by extending investment planning on a rigorous, simplified, objective client-driven, and low fixed-fee basis to individual investors with my new-era advisory firm. I will also provide guidance for evaluating or engaging investment advisors to help optimize your relationship with them for those who believe that their advisor adds measurable value to their account.

Individual investors need not engage in any fee-based service if they understand the nature of equity markets and their emotional resilience to what is often a volatile experience in stocks. The do-it-yourself approach can be challenging, and perhaps more so without coaching by a paid advisor but is still a perfectly viable way to invest your money—and a very gratifying experience if one establishes and follows simple rules.

I realize that the leap from a wealth management relationship with ongoing fees to a do-it-yourself approach may be difficult, which is why I have established a fixed-fee consultative service that is uncommon, for the reasons enumerated, that keep people committed to their investment advisors.

Summary

- My mission is to increase awareness that there are more attractive and profitable investment approaches for the individual investor than the investment management industry, which can reduce the anxiety of investing.
- Benefit individual investors with a simple, but not simplistic approach with the advantage of low fixed fees for investment advice and coaching.
- The investment management industry is entrenched and relies largely on the public's lack of knowledge of the investment process. Their actual role is not unlike the wizard in *The Wonderful Wizard of Oz*.

WHERE ARE WE TODAY?

TECHNOLOGICAL ADVANCES AND COMPETITION have afforded all investors efficient access to prudent, diversified, low-cost liquid investment vehicles and services that can give them control and the significant benefit of very low fees. Importantly, this includes those with relatively small sums to invest. The improvement in quality and scope of web-based investment resources, which were not available until the early 2000s, has increased exponentially since I started my former firm in May 1995. As surprising as this may be, Microsoft had not embraced the Internet in the spring of 1995! The software applications that my firm used were still delivered on small floppy discs that had very limited capacity. Of course, Microsoft applications were delivered on physical media, which were upgraded at least every few years, requiring new purchases and installation on local servers or PCs. Those processes now seem like we were wearing bearskins and working with stone axes and figuratively, we were! No applications were integrated, so we needed to acquire several separate platforms to get stock market data, investment manager profiles and performance data, mutual fund data, asset allocation modeling, and client reporting. It was labor-intensive and no doubt will become exponentially more efficient with the advent of Artificial Intelligence. The costs are now less than one-tenth of what they were in 1995, and the performance of the applications has improved at least tenfold.

What individual investors can do now

It is not a full-time job to invest independently today. Easy access to efficient investment vehicles is available to all investors at blended total portfolio fees that use Exchange Traded Funds (ETFs) and even managed mutual funds for much less than the typical registered investment advisory firm or so-called wealth management firm. Advisors should happily disclose the total fees that a client pays their firm and those fees that underlying funds in the portfolio may charge.

The importance of compounding cannot be over-emphasized, so here is another example of what it means in dollars and cents. For clarity, let us assume that a hypothetical individual has $100,000 to invest and engages an advisor who charges 1% of assets, so the annual, initial fee is $1,000 but will increase with the value of the portfolio. For comparative purposes, let us further assume that investor earns 6% a year before the advisor's fee and the various charges of any funds in which they invest, which can be from zero to well over 1% per year based on asset value, but the 6% would be earned after portfolio constituent fund fees and before the advisor fee of 1%. The value of the $100,000 after ten years at a 6% rate, compounded annually, would be $179,085. The same $100,000 at a 5% rate would compound to $162,889 in ten years. One percent may not sound like much, but when compounded is significant and yields a 10% increase in final value in ten years. Further let us assume that the *all-in* advisor fee is 0.30%, which in practice is a very low aggregate fee but one that many Internet-based advisory services charge in addition to fees charged by funds in which they invest, as well as fees that they may collect from mutual funds. If that investor earns 5.7% a year for ten years, the final value would be $174,080, or $5,005 less than a 6% annualized return. Fees matter—a lot and can be controlled with certainty, unlike all other variables present in investing.

In addition to legacy registered investment advisory arrangements, there are automated, so-called robo-investment advisory firms that offer to manage portfolios that receive fees that are usually more than 0.30% when all compensation is considered. It happens that such robo firms may direct their clients to invest in mutual funds for which they receive a portion of the fees, termed 12 (b) 1 fees in the industry, and paid as a marketing expense by the mutual fund to the investment advisor. Of course, there are firms that one can find easily with an Internet search that will recommend supposedly suitable investment advisory firms and receive a solicitation fee for such recommendations. These firms usually assess investor suitability with a few simple multiple-choice questions that usually are submitted with the inquirer's contact information as favored by investment industry regulators to establish suitability. Such firms may not advertise the compensation arrangements with the firms that they recommend, although they can be found in the disclaimers. The obvious problem with such recommendations is that they may well offer *adverse selection*, which is to say that they only recommend those firms that have agreed to pay them referral fees, not all the firms that may be suitable for the inquiring prospect. One might also inquire about what due diligence and other criteria the recommending firms require. The average investor should do their own due diligence analysis. The typical questions that an investor should ask a prospective advisor are included in the due diligence questionnaire in the last chapter.

Investment portfolios are part of an individual's financial plan and as mentioned individuals may need the advice of a financial planner for a review of their retirement, tax and estate planning, and insurance coverage, but not necessarily an investment advisor that charges 0.8% a year or more of the client's assets under management. Consulting services that address the average investor's need to establish an investment plan, a statement of investment objectives, and a structured, disciplined, typically quarterly review process are what institutional investors have used for years as their most trusted advisors. My former firm offered such consulting services. The idea is to pay for what you use, not for someone sitting on the bench collecting fees every day whether they perform daily value-added functions or not. Unless an advisor is managing individual securities and can demonstrate the value that they have added above a relevant index benchmark, there is no reason to pay premium asset-based annual fees that are typically 1% of assets that they manage. The market has spoken loudly in the past twenty or so years by moving assets to index strategies with very low or even no fees—and the investors who have done so have performed in line with broad index benchmarks with the certainty of fee savings.

Investment planning and strategy are the foundation of a successful program, which is where investors should concentrate their initial efforts. The most important part of the planning process is to reconcile one's tolerance for the risk of losing value, against the need to maintain purchasing power and/or enhance value in the long term. This obviously means that investors must successfully pass the tests that the financial markets inevitably throw at them to succeed in the long term. Any investment strategy will be tested by the market. All investors should plan to review their strategy annually with at least quarterly monitoring of their progress. It does not require daily fee-based supervision of a properly diversified portfolio if one is truly a long-term investor. Understanding the basic principles of maintaining the purchasing power of one's assets is essential. It is also essential to acknowledge that saving fees is a non-trivial component of a successful investment program. I say this again because more than a few people with advisors trivialize or perhaps rationalize the fees that they pay.

I will not dive into the academic theory of interest rates and why they historically have been positive. Let us assume that the long history of positive interest rates will continue if there is demand for money and credit. Indeed, after the Great Financial Crisis of 2008-2009 interest rates in many countries were negative when investors actually paid a bank or borrower of their funds to accept their investment. Some mortgages in European countries actually paid interest to those who mortgaged their homes in the negative interest rate environment. It is very difficult to accept the concept of negative interest rates, but a significant portion of government debt in some countries meant that investors paid interest to own those bonds rather than receiving interest payments from them. It is hard to imagine, but true. Interest rates in the U.S. were very low or close to zero during this post-Great Financial Crisis interval, until early 2022, and investors were highly incentivized to assume risk to generate a return.

In March 2022, the Federal Reserve Bank's Open Market Committee decided to begin increasing the Federal Funds Rate that banks pay or are paid for overnight lending or borrowing. Indeed, until March 2022 the low to zero interest rate policy of the U.S. Federal Reserve Bank was termed "financial repression" that forced investors to assume risk, or to earn essentially no return because interest rates were so low. It happens that returns to those who assumed risk during this period were well-rewarded as equity markets rose to all-time high levels through the end of 2021, and bonds until the summer of 2020 produced good total returns as their prices advanced with lower yields to maturity.

The Major Impediment to Efficient Investment Freedom

I believe that many individual investors are intimidated and probably feel overwhelmed by the risk of investing and the anxiety that it may cause. So, they buy into the hustle. To me, it is a statement that the industry has people drinking its Kool-Aid, not thinking independently, and not educating people, but is merely selling them based on their fears. As detailed above, if one knows the fees that they pay and finds that they are acceptable for the value delivered, that is fine, but most do not if my years of anecdotal and quantitative information are correct. It is my effort to excite transparency in an industry that does not necessarily plainly disclose all options to investors. Several of the largest firms in the industry have delivered investment vehicles that democratize investing, but people are slow to take advantage of the opportunity although their advisors probably have. Adoption may take years, to the detriment of thousands of asset-based, fee-paying investment advisory clients with long-term strategies who are essentially captives of those firms. At the very least, the due diligence questions that all investors should ask may be beneficial to them in the short and long term. Pay only for what you get.

My primary goal as an institutional investor was to keep clients on track with their respective strategies, which were predicated on holding stocks for the long term. This was not always easy because financial behavior tends to repeat itself. It tends to swing between fear and greed, and while that may seem a harsh description it is no less true. Clients would naturally become more concerned about their portfolios after a steep stock market decline and question why they had taken such a risk. My job was to help investors determine their risk tolerance before they exceeded this level.

Our core equity allocations at my former firm included index funds. In addition to fixed income allocations to modulate volatility, we included a variety of strategies that exploited opportunity in inefficiently priced financial market verticals. Such sectors, and investment managers or hedge funds, typically were too small for the large institutional investors, thus providing opportunities. Those allocations required significant research and due diligence and were available only to qualified purchasers who had at least five million dollars in liquid assets, so are beyond the scope of the basic message of this book. Hedge fund allocations are not necessary for those with long-term investment horizons. Yes, skilled managers receive a lot of publicity, but their services are not usually available to the typical individual investor.

Summary

- Technology and competition have leveled the playing field for individual investors to gain access to efficient investment vehicles and information at low fees.
- Do not be intimidated by the investment process and think independently.

ELIMINATE INVESTMENT ANXIETY

Questions That Investors Must Ask Advisors, or as Yogi Berra said, "You can observe a lot by just watching."

YES, ELIMINATE ANXIETY ABOUT INVESTING. When we know what to expect within clear boundaries, our concerns or anxiety should be lowered or even eliminated. Investors must focus on planning to understand the implications of potential return and risk. If you are a stock investor, how do you feel when the market falls, either gradually or suddenly, by a significant amount and stays down for over a year? If you have endured and can endure such declines without a visceral reaction, and you have not made emotionally driven changes in your portfolio exposure, this book will reinforce your resolve.

Your biggest investment costs are missing opportunities in the stock market and paying annual fees to an advisor. The larger of the two costs is an emotional reaction to a market decline that causes an investor to vacate, or significantly reduce exposure to stocks, and not participate in a recovery. Stock market recoveries have been dramatic and historically have occurred when the business and economic outlook had appeared likely to deteriorate further, feeding concerns that the stock slide would continue.

The second biggest cost is paying an investment advisor every day for the rest of your life, based on annual asset-based fees that will increase as your portfolio value increases. You should only pay for value that you get, not for the apparent comfort of full-time engagement with an advisor, who unless the advisor is super-human, does not know what the stock market will do in the short- or even intermediate-term anymore than an everyday person. Check the advisor's batting average on successful stock market predictions if you doubt my assertion. You can check their documented and regulatory-compliant performance record of stock market predictions that they should provide for your review. I am not advocating that you immediately release your investment advisor, but I am urging you to understand exactly how the advisor adds value after the fees. Should the advisor satisfactorily answer the questions that will reveal how they add value then your relationship with the advisor may improve. At the very least you will have a better idea of why you are paying fees—and what you are getting in return.

Other costs include not thinking independently, believing that only professional advisors can understand the stock market, not establishing risk and return preferences (including the maximum decline tolerable), and not adhering to a structure and framework of objective and regular review. As simple as it may seem, a disciplined quarterly or more frequent review is a structural advantage.

Let's Just Buy Low and Sell High!

If your investment horizon is long-term, you need not assume the risk of trying to time your exposure to the stock market, and it is best to stay invested. You may do it yourself or ask your advisor to make modest changes to allocations depending on solid criteria, but major changes are unnecessary unless you change your objective.

Consistent short-term stock market prediction is a low probability of a successful endeavor. Therefore, the prudent and conventional advice, which is perfectly valid, is to stay the course and maintain your equity allocation after a decline in the market. Is this advice for which you should pay someone daily for the rest of your life? I think not. If you believe that it is, then you should ask your advisor to tabulate the cumulative fees that you have paid, and then ask them to calculate the likely future fees. It is also a good idea to ask the advisor to calculate the dollar value that would have been generated had your portfolio been invested in market indices in proportion to your actual investments. The numbers may surprise you.

How can I be so sure that my advice to stay invested is the best? Obviously, nobody can predict the future with certainty, but we can assign probabilities to outcomes in the future based on past financial behavior and how it manifested itself at market levels. A bold promise and one that happens to be mathematically and probabilistically true at this point in history and probably for much longer in the future. The reason is basically that the prices of financial assets reflect investor behavior, which tends to repeat itself. Institutional investors for years have relied on this tendency to preserve the value of their assets after inflation. This book does not promise to reveal a secret sauce or a path to rapid wealth. It bases the projection of 95% certainly on history. Of course, the other 5% of the time the outcome may fall well outside of the 95% probability. As you will see, it is prudent to explore scenarios that may lie outside of the 95% range, and that is part of the process of investing with confidence, and with little or no fear, as I will describe. I realize that many investment books promise a lot, but this promise is a practical solution based on the tendency of stocks to display a propensity to return to their mean or average returns in high single digits over time. I am well aware of the familiar tendency to simply extrapolate recent market behavior, either positive or negative into the future but the point of planning is to anticipate the reasonable range of outcomes over various time horizons.

Commentators may argue that the past is not a good indication of the future and that returns to equity investors will be much lower than in the past, with usually eloquent arguments citing a variety of financial and economic factors. They probably do not invest your money so are not accountable for their predictions. In fairness to the negative view of prospective equity returns, the last fifty years have seen a major increase in the money supply and inflation that may not persist in the future. During that time, the S&P 500 had a total return of a bit over 10% a year on average, albeit with several dramatic and prolonged declines. The economy may stop growing at even a nominal pace, and any number of other potentially negative factors will undoubtedly confront us. The most recent interval of economic and financial stress was due to the pandemic that led to supply chain disruptions, and other factors, as well as an extraordinary increase in the money supply and fiscal policies designed to support demand. We also experienced meaningfully higher consumer price inflation. During times of financial market duress, many seek guidance or reassurance, and the financial media is happy to offer such commentators. It may be difficult to avoid the media's sometimes fearful, short-term messages about the financial markets, but it is vital to maintain your individual perspective about the longer-term prospects. Fear can be a powerful motivator, which probably explains why so many who get media attention emphasize negatives.

It is essential for investors to objectively determine their return and risk preferences, and then develop a strategy that has the highest probability of achieving the desired outcome at different points in the future, and also after considering other factors like the level of future contributions, future payments, inflation, and the time horizon.

I suggest a simple framework designed to save investors thousands of dollars in fees while delivering the confidence necessary to be resolute about an investment plan. I am passionate about the investment process and am compelled to share my views on it for the benefit of others, and I also accept that my views may conflict with conventional and well-entrenched practices. The practice of charging annual investment advisory fees based on a percentage of the portfolio asset value is likely to be defended by investment advisors but is not necessarily congruent with the services that they provide. Specifically, why should you pay for daily advice under such an arrangement, when the advisor typically devotes little or no time daily supervising or managing your portfolio? If your strategy is long-term there is little reason to make frequent changes to its allocations. Once your strategy is established, and the portfolio is invested, the best advice has always been to stay the course through stock market downturns. Most clients contact their advisors when they are concerned about negative financial market events, and good practice by advisors has been to reassure their clients that a longer-term posture is likely to achieve their goals rather than trying to exit and then reenter the positions.

The legacy practices of investors and advisors can benefit from changes made possible by competitive and technological advances, if they are open to a simpler and better way to plan and manage investments. We can control our costs, but not the financial markets, so let us start by controlling our costs and by establishing realistic and specific probability parameters for our portfolios. Investment risk and cost management with clear expectations are at the center of the process that I advocate. I advocate a consultative, fixed-fee approach to objectively establish your investment return and risk preferences, and then structure a portfolio that aligns with your risk tolerance. The tools that I use now, and used at my former firm, offer an extremely efficient way to objectively determine a client's risk and return preferences, and an analysis of the existing portfolio to determine if it aligns with the client's risk parameters. It also produces a detailed series of portfolio exhibits and risk/return probability analysis, including an investment policy statement. Institutions have used consultants under fixed fee and/or low-fee arrangements for many years, and it is the type of advice that I delivered to my clients for twenty-five years with my own firm.

This book is intended for investors with long-term horizons who want to optimize their investment plan and its implementation, not day traders or those who aspire to make significant short-term gains in the stock market. Let us start with a detailed review of the catalyst for me to write this book. As mentioned previously, several friends and acquaintances have asked me what they should do with their investments since I retired. These friends had between a few hundred thousand and a few million dollars in their portfolios. Rather than try to determine their preferences, I suggested that they ask their incumbent investment advisor a few questions.

Questions to which investors did not have answers but should

My **first question** to them was if they engaged an investment advisor. All answered, yes.

The **second question** that I asked is how much and when they pay their advisor. Surprising but true: Although investors who pay advisors may know the price of typical daily and annual goods and services, most who have engaged me in conversation about their investments do not know how much they pay their advisors, and even tell me that they do not care because their advisor takes the burden of decisions off them and that their portfolios have appreciated.

My respondents all said that they did not know how and when their advisor got paid. I suggested that they might want to ask their advisors for a tabulation of the fees that they paid, and what percentage the cumulative amount of fees represents as a percentage of their current portfolio value. Then ask their advisors to calculate how much dollar value they have added, more than a market index return, after their fees since they began managing the portfolio. The advisor should be happy to comply and if not, then the answer is probably clear. One individual said that asking their advisor about fees would be confrontational. I do not know what explains that mindset, but it could be that the individual was intimidated by the entire process and just defaulted to the advisor, without inquiry, as a path of least resistance. In my world, one should understand what they pay for, when, and what they can expect to receive in value. They should also be informed that the regulations require that advisory fees be negotiable, so ask for a lower fee. In this instance, it was a real estate broker who did not want to ask about fees or negotiate a lower fee, which is odd because negotiation is at the core of a real estate broker's role professionally. It suggests that this person was intimidated, which is in my experience incongruent with real estate brokers but says a lot about this client's mindset about how they value their advisor.

One of those I asked, a retired trial lawyer, had no idea of what he paid in fees over many years but was quick to add that he enjoyed the annual advisor-sponsored outing to the polo matches.

He allowed that he should probably "cross-examine" his advisor.

Let us put aside, at least for the moment, the ubiquitous aspirational advertisements with videos of people enjoying themselves in ideal backdrops that regale us from the investment industry that suggest desirable outcomes and invitations to engage with them for solutions, so that you too can have an ideal future with your money. Or for that matter the firms that claim to be different because they "only" charge fees based on assets that they manage, and that they only do better when you do better. They fail to say that they make money when their clients lose value in their accounts. Sure, when the stock market goes up those firms get more fees, but how does that benefit their customers? Have they done more work to deserve higher fees because of stock market strength? Do they give fees back when the stock market declines? Do their advertisements make it clear that our regulatory laws require them to be fiduciaries and to put the client's interests first, and that all registered investment advisors are fiduciaries? If they do not, they should make such a disclosure. They should also disclose that the regulations stipulate that fees are negotiable, which they never do in their video advertisements.

The **third question** was how frequently the advisor made changes to their portfolio. They said that they did not know but thought that there were very few transactions, if any, over the course of a year. I did not press anyone for more specific answers about portfolio activity because it was immediately obvious that they were not comfortable talking about the details of their portfolios, and in any event, I told them that I was not offering investment advice, only questions, the answers to which would inform them.

My **fourth question** was whether their advisor reported their rates of return relative to their objectives and compared them to index benchmarks that replicated their asset allocation in regular quarterly reports. They all said no, which was hard for me to believe, but they did not recall such reports or comparisons. Perhaps their failure to remember performance reports is that they do not focus on their quarterly statements or performance reports. The tendency of investors not to focus on their portfolio reports is common in my experience and might be attributable to inertia surrounding decisions about their money. It may also be attributable to the difficulty of understanding the reports.

The **fifth question** was whether they had ever asked their advisor to explain how she or he added value to their portfolio and if so to explain how the advisor objectively measured the added value. I hesitated to ask how the advisor described its structural advantages, but that is a due diligence question in a list contained in a later chapter. None had asked those questions or knew the answers.

The **sixth question** was whether their advisor had helped them to determine their strategy and goals, and most importantly to define explicitly in dollar terms what was the likely risk of asset value decline that they may experience over both short and long-term time horizons. None had received such explicit advice.

The **seventh question** I asked was whether they had a statement of investment policy, objectives, and restrictions and reviewed it at least annually with their advisor. None had received such a document or periodic review, also a bit hard for me to believe, but that was their recollection.

Finally, I asked them if they were happy with their advisor. All said that they were happy and that their advisor had made them "a lot of money," although none had any comparison to what "a lot" meant, in what has been a very productive financial market environment for years, where just owning a low or no-cost index fund also made "a lot" of money. I did not ask them what "a lot" meant relative to what they might have generated with a simple portfolio of index funds, as I did not want to risk embarrassing any of them.

If your advisor offers satisfactory answers to all the above, then you are in a rare group and are or should be understandably satisfied with their services.

It was blindingly clear from the conversations that most people do not want to confront the reality of their money and find it easier to delegate all decisions to a registered advisory firm. The deliberate avoidance of asking simple questions, as outlined in the previous paragraphs, is a statement of several factors, not the least is that inertia and procrastination easily overcome inquisitiveness regarding personal investment plans. As Charles Dickens said, "Procrastination is the thief of time." It is that very inertia on which the investment advisory community depends for its "sticky assets under management." It also suggests that the advertising of advisory services is extremely effective, without ever explicitly describing the annual cost of a typical portfolio or the multi-year amount of fees, and how they relate to any value added.

I believe that my observations are representative of at least a portion, if not most of the individual investor community. Most investors and their advisors execute long-term strategies, so make few changes in a year. Remember that Warren Buffett's favorite holding period is "forever." Sure, the advisor may rebalance their asset allocation if there is a significant advance or decline in stock or bond markets, but those are infrequent. They may also wish to harvest tax losses near year-end, but this is only for taxable accounts, not retirement accounts like IRAs and 401(k)s, and in any event, is likely not a significant value add. Ask the advisor to describe the percentage tax drag of your portfolio, for example, if they make a big deal about their tax loss harvesting ability. Tax drag means that if one realizes gains and pays taxes on those gains, the amount available for reinvestment is less, which reduces the compounding impact of an investment that is held for the long term. Our application calculates tax drag and so should your advisor's.

My respondents' advisors invest their portfolios based on what the advisor believes is a suitable objective and risk profile, usually described with subjective terms like "conservative," income-oriented," "moderate growth," or "aggressive." Those terms can mean vastly different things to different people, and generalizations about one's money may not be helpful. *Close-enough to me is not a strategy description for real money plans.* Basically, the asset-based annual fees charged, which grow in dollars as the portfolio appreciates, require very little incremental time, if any, or effort for an advisor, and except for perhaps a few hours of initial setup work the advisor has little to do except occasionally call the client, or send regulatory required quarterly reports. For that, they are paid an annual fee that accrues daily.

My simple proposition is to pay for risk and return preference determination objectively and definitively, not subjectively, and pay for portfolio strategy and at least initial portfolio composition *only once*, not every day and year. ***How many times should anyone pay for the same advice multiple times when there is no reason to change strategy or its implementation?*** The advisor will tell clients that it has continuous supervisory responsibility over the portfolio, and so they do, but if clients are concerned about the fluctuation in value on an intraday or less frequent interval, they can set up price alerts at their brokerage or custody firm for their portfolio. Apparently, it is the unquantifiable comfort factor to which people are conditioned and pay without a clear idea of the value that they get. More likely, the client is led to believe that the legacy, annual fee based on assets under management approach is the only one offered, and it is suitable for them.

Individuals can employ the same investment principles used by their advisors and do so with significant resources that are easily accessible from major brokerage firms and mutual fund complexes, for little or no cost. This was not always the case, but technology and competition have changed the landscape in favor of everyday investors. *What has not changed meaningfully are the annual asset-based, ongoing fees that advisors charge.* The fundamental principle of investing adopted by advisors is that financial behavior will respond to short-term factors sometimes dramatically, but over longer time periods reflect the fundamental values of stocks and bonds. While that may sound complicated, it is quite simple, as I will explore and explain. One of my rules in life and investing is to keep things simple, although not simplistic.

Engaging advisors may seem like a simple solution to concerns about investing, and its well-worn path offers apparent comfort that many investors seek. The benefits are reinforced very effectively through advertising, which astonishingly never discusses the objective value of their advisory services. We just must take their word for it that they add significant value to our lives. The reality is that no matter how large the advisory firm is, it does not control the course of financial markets. Nor has their shorter-term predictive ability about the markets been either consistently accurate or insightful in my experience. We can put our own money at risk just as the advisors do if we arm ourselves with knowledge about how to determine our objectives and manage our own investment program. The rewards of our efforts will go well beyond just saving fees.

More about my practical experience and how it reinforces my conviction

It is said that experience is what one gets when one does not get what he or she wants. It is also true that successful outcomes offer valuable experience, reinforce disciplined thinking, and adherence to simple rules and habits.

It has also been said that you should not find out who you are in the stock market. This may seem a flippant assertion but is at the core of a lesson that every investor should learn. I am not sure to whom to attribute this statement but recall it from a long-ago reading of James Grant's biography of Bernard Baruch, the well-known stock speculator of the 1920s. Anyway, throughout this book let us explore who you are in terms of investing and do so on an informed and objective basis.

It was my responsibility to answer the question of whether advisors were adding value for twenty-five years with my own firm, as an advisor to endowment funds and family investment offices. The stubborn fact is that it was and is uncommon for advisors to add significant value after their fees, compared to popular relevant market index performance on a persistent basis. I believe that the sense of comfort that many investors have with advisors is based on the likeability of the advisor and/or size of the firm and its apparent acumen and sophistication, but rarely if ever on objective performance measurement after fees. Perhaps the investor thinks that if a firm is exceptionally large and has an established name that is reinforced with nearly ubiquitous brand advertising that it must be good. Or is it an emperor has new clothes phenomenon, where if enough people believe it, it must be true? I believe that it is the latter, and the fact that the stock market over time has produced gains is the dominant factor in people's perception of value added by advisors. They believe that were it not for advisors, they may not have owned stocks or have maintained their allocations when confronted with a market decline. The discipline to remain invested in stocks after a decline offers the highest probability of a desirable outcome, and I will describe a proven approach to gain this confidence. It is axiomatic that every strategy will be tested, and it is the ability to withstand the test that defines desirable outcomes. As already emphatically stated, it is the need to know one's tolerance risk before it is exceeded that defines desired long-term investment outcomes.

THE DIMINISHED PURCHASING
POWER OF THE DOLLAR

IT IS COINCIDENTAL that I started my investment career in August 1971, the same month President Nixon suspended the convertibility of the U.S. dollar to gold to stabilize the economy. This is important because it led to a significant expansion in our money supply by the Federal Reserve Bank, commonly referred to as the "Fed," and to the extraordinary loss of purchasing power of the U.S. dollar. Its Congressional mandate is to execute policies that maintain full employment and stable inflation. It has the authority to issue dollars and regulate credit. The Fed creates dollars by fiat. That means that it creates dollars out of thin air. The various Fed officials who issue statements about their policy rarely, if ever, say this out loud, but it is no less true. Of course, the Fed members convene regularly, make regular announcements about its policies, and have a large staff of PhDs as a resource, but the bottom line is that they create money by fiat, which means that they create dollars at will. I believe that it is confidence in our system of government, the robust U.S. economy, and the powerful military that are the primary reasons that the dollar is the reserve currency for global trade and exchange, despite its significant decline in purchasing power.

Fiat currencies of other countries and regions, such as the European Union that sponsors the euro, have also lost purchasing power. Currencies in recently prosperous countries have lost most of their value in just the last few years, as savers lost confidence in the central banks of those countries and/or governments and economies. For example, Venezuela and Lebanon have seen the value of their currencies decline precipitously, nearly wiping out the value of savings accounts in those currencies. The most well-known currency failure is that of the Weimar Republic in Germany. One hundred years ago in 1923, the German government printed currency to pay striking workers. A loaf of bread that cost 250 marks in January 1923 rose to 200,000 *million* marks (lots of zeros) by November 1923. Such an increase is unfathomable, but true. The slow-motion depreciation of the dollar's purchasing power does not alarm people, but it is still pernicious.

What is so significant about the U.S. abandoning gold convertibility? The increase in the money supply growth rate beginning in 1971 led to the most persistent decline of the purchasing power of the U.S. dollar since its creation by the Fed in 1913. One dollar's worth of goods in 1971 cost about $7.68 in mid-2023 based on the U.S. Consumer Price Index as reported by the U.S. Bureau of Labor Statistics, or 13% of what it did in 1971. That was a decline of 3.8% a year in purchasing power, or 87%. Over the same fifty-two years, the stock market has produced rates of return despite periodic significant declines at a total annualized rate of return of 10.5% for the S&P 500, with dividends reinvested and no tax through the end of 2022. Taxpayers must pay taxes on dividends, so did not compound their assets by investing in the S&P 500 at 10.5%. The reason for using the 10.5% rate is that pension funds, like a 401(k) or Individual Retirement Account (IRA) compound at a tax-free rate with dividends reinvested. Of course, taxes, either long-term capital gains or ordinary income, can reduce returns materially. One can assume that long-term gains taxes will reduce returns by about one-fifth, while ordinary income can reduce returns by about a third.

From August 1971 to year end 2022, the *after-inflation* annualized rate of return for the S&P 500, with dividends reinvested but without tax, was 6.3%. To keep this illustration clear, one dollar invested in the S&P 500 with dividends reinvested and no tax at the 10.5% annualized rate that it delivered, which would have been the case in a qualified retirement plan, would have grown to $170! And that does not assume that any funds were added to the investment, that would have been true if it were a retirement savings plan. One 1971 dollar saved in a jar would buy $0.13 now. The choice in retrospect is clear. Einstein was right about the power of compound interest as the Eighth Wonder of the World.

A brief look at interest rate history illustrates the financial market response to Fed policy. Interest rates have gone from their September 1981 high yield to maturity of 15.84% on Ten Year U.S. Treasury Notes, to their low of 0.55% in July 2020. (Source: St. Louis Federal Reserve Bank.) The yield to maturity has since increased to about 4.3% as of this writing in December 2023. Returns to bond investors over the fifty-two years were less than those of stocks, despite the longest bull market in bonds in history. (Bonds increase in principle value as yields to maturity decline.) One could have significantly increased the buying power of their dollars by investing in common stocks with some diversification into bonds during the decline in interest rates. Indeed, it is not unreasonable to observe that the Fed's monetary policy during the decline from historic high yields on bonds since late 1981 created an incentive for investors to own common stocks. In recent years this has been termed "financial repression," as incredibly low bond and short-term interest rates were insufficient to satisfy the investment goals of most investors.

The old axiom to not fight the Fed has value. Although common today, stock investing did not become popular among everyday people until well after 1971. Stock investing has become much more accessible, efficient, and lower cost in recent years, and it is recognized as a reasonable long-term hedge against the loss of purchasing power in the future by many.

Summary

- Price inflation is insidious and very harmful to asset values, especially over longer time horizons.
- History has demonstrated that the best long-term way for individual investors to preserve their purchasing power is by owning a representative stock index, such as the S&P 500 Composite Stock Index.

WHAT IS RISK?

RISK AND UNCERTAINTY are not necessarily synonymous. Risk can be quantified with probability analysis, while uncertainty involves unknown probabilities and unpredictable outcomes. We have more information with which to assess risk, while uncertainty requires more flexibility to confront situations with limited information or history.

We will address the obvious investment risks but also want to recognize the implications of risks in our daily lives compared to investment risks. The primary risk for investors is the permanent loss of part or all their capital. Before proceeding, let us consider that losing 50% of one's value requires a 100% increase to break even. So of course, limiting declines can be a seductive promise for an investment strategy. Given the difficulty of successfully executing such strategies, holding stocks after market declines has been a productive strategy for long-term investors, even if it appears to be very risky. I advocate that investors understand the risks of a financial market decline, and that they calibrate their portfolios to align with their particular risk tolerance to deter them from selling after a decline.

Diversification is the easiest way to hedge against, but not eliminate, risk; just as concentrating allocations can lead to the most profitable outcomes, with the attendant risk of losing more. The primary risk of permanent loss is followed by how far a portfolio can fall in value within a fixed period before the investor capitulates and makes a fear-based decision.

Investment risk can include:

- Losing money permanently, not just through periodic declines in value.
- Not adhering to a long-term strategy after a stock market decline.
- Not avoiding the familiar temptation to follow the crowd after significant increases in price.
- Ignoring the fact that past performance may not be indicative of future performance.
- The risk of affinity investing or following others whom you may know or respect.
- Not thinking and acting independently.
- Not generating sufficient returns relative to our goals.
- Accepting fraudulent offerings.
- Determining the wrong investment time horizon.
- Incurring taxes on gains that leave less to reinvest after paying taxes.

We have a variety of risks in our lives and how we personally define them matters because the risk to one person may not be a risk to another, and if it is it may be to a far different degree. Perhaps the most important risk in life is the chance, or probability, that a person will be physically harmed or experience an adverse health effect if exposed to a hazard, and one that we take precautions to avoid. Pay attention while driving and take care not to swim beyond our ability to return to safety, for example. *We know the rules.* In addition to financial risks, there are certainly other risks to us, our families, and our social well-being. We adopt our own framework of risk management to live safely and productively in our daily lives, and we should do so with our investments with the same focus.

While this book is about understanding and managing investment risk, it is important to note how we live with other risks in our lives and how we minimize or eliminate them. How we manage our everyday risks with our habits, routines, customs, and conventions should be a lesson about how we may view various investment risks. Our habits and customs bring order to what may be chaotic or random circumstances. Most of us adopt routines, customs, or habits in our daily lives intended to reduce the risks to our physical well-being, maximize our peace of mind, and joy. Society has conventions and laws that govern our ability to take risks and because of this, we have expectations of how others will behave. Although we may not focus on our own framework of actions or routines and behavior to minimize potential personal harm, our own protocol is a framework of rules that we follow to avoid unpleasant outcomes to our health and well-being. When we deviate from our routine or rules, we know that we are elevating the chance of an undesirable outcome or outright harm to our physical or financial health. How many times have you bent your own rules even a little bit, and then regretted your actions? Oh, no problem, there is nobody around so I can just roll through this stop sign. Rules and customs matter in almost all areas of our lives.

Before launching into the technical definitions of measures of investment risk that academia has developed to explain certain aspects of a security's behavior, it is vital to underscore that all the measures are based on a market benchmark. There is value in the various measures of risk-adjusted return metrics, but for most of us, they are an unnecessary complication. Notice how the terms in the investment industry may be confusing to most people, but they have given many the opportunity to justify their analysis in a shorthand way, without considering the *qualitative* factors that affect the future performance of a strategy. While interesting, the measures described below could provide insight into an inquiry about qualitative factors of a strategy, but by themselves are of limited use. Qualitative factors determine the value of a strategy or investment manager. Past performance may reveal strengths and weaknesses so is useful in evaluating a strategy. One may have reservations about extrapolating past performance into the future, but provided that the investment process is consistently practiced it is the best that we have, as it is unlikely that we can predict the future with at least modest certainty without considering past financial behavior that is reflected in rates of return. In my opinion, financial market behavior is rational in the long term, although subject to emotional responses and volatility on a short to intermediate-term basis. What does the intermediate term mean? To me two to five or so years. Ten years is the most common time horizon for those who invest entirely in stocks. Most investors reduce equity risk by allocating part of their assets to bonds that have been, until 2022 when interest rates increased significantly and rapidly causing bond prices to decline, an efficient way to diversify equity risk.

The benchmark upon which most comparative measures of investment success are based is the S&P 500 Composite Stock Price Index. It is a widely accepted, diversified equity portfolio. Most professional investors use it as a broad benchmark and try to outperform its return with less volatility. One of the main points of this book is that if one invests in the benchmark, in this case, the S&P 500, it represents the relative goal that professionals endeavor to exceed. Therefore, why not just invest in the S&P 500 where we can save fees? Although dependent upon the time interval used for relative measurement, it is unusual for a manager to outperform the S&P 500 consistently, not just in terms of the net rate of return, but the volatility of the return. Without getting too technical, the S&P 500 is a capitalization-weighted index of stocks of companies that have certain characteristics deemed attractive to the Standard and Poor's stock selection committee. The index represents those companies that have succeeded and attracted investor capital so weighs the most successful more heavily than the smaller capitalized company stocks. Of course, smaller capitalized companies can be profitable, and the most successful ones grow large enough to be included in the S&P 500. The Index is weighted heavily to the largest companies, with only ten of the largest holdings, or 2% of the index constituents, of the largest company stocks now representing 30% of the index. It may not be the best gauge at times when smaller capitalized stocks perform very well, and over an extended period, an equal-weighted S&P 500 has outperformed the popular, capitalization-weighted index. In the thirty years that ended June 30, 2023, for example, the capitalization-weighted S&P 500 had an annualized total rate of return of 10.04%, while the equal-weighted S&P 500 generated a total annualized rate of return of 10.91%. The 0.87% annual difference may seem like a trivial difference to many, but $100,000 invested for thirty years in the capitalization-weighted S&P 500 would have grown to $1,764,077, while the same amount invested in the equal-weighted S&P 500 Index would have grown to $2,243,195, or 27.1% more money. For perspective, when we talk about the value of the one-percentage-point that most pay their advisors, we are talking about real money, not a trivial amount when compounded.

What are risk-adjusted rates of return? Risk-adjusted rates of return reflect the level of risk expressed as the standard deviation from the mean, or volatility incurred for a unit of return.

Institutional investors often refer to risk-adjusted rates of return when comparing strategies that they may be evaluating for use to determine if the return generated justified the level of risk. All such metrics assume the consistency of processes, or factors that influence historical returns, and not the previously mentioned qualitative factors. Although there are a variety of metrics, the various measures described below are only one method of evaluating the effectiveness of a particular strategy.

The most common methods to calculate risk-adjusted rates of return include:

- **Alpha:** A measure of how much value a portfolio manager or an investment strategy has added or subtracted relative to a designated benchmark index or the overall market. The formula: Alpha = Actual Return - ((Market Return - Risk-Free Rate)). The risk-free rate is typically that of 13-week (91-day) U.S. Treasury Bills, most often referred to as the "Three-month Treasury Bill." If alpha is positive the investment has outperformed its expected return given its level of risk. Negative alpha indicates underperformance. Among the various metrics of investment performance, the most important one after the net rate of return is to know this metric when evaluating advisors.

- **Beta:** A measure of a stock or investment's volatility in relation to the overall market. It is a statistical measure that helps investors understand how much an individual asset tends to move in response to fluctuations in the broader market. The beta coefficient is typically calculated by analyzing historical price data of the asset in question and comparing it to a benchmark index, such as the S&P 500 for the U.S. market.

The benchmark index is assigned a beta of 1.0, representing the average market movement. An asset with a beta greater than 1.0 is more volatile than the market, while an asset with a beta less than 1.0 is less volatile. Negative Beta: In some cases, an asset may have a negative beta. This means it moves in the opposite direction of the market. When the market goes up, this asset tends to decline, and vice versa. Negative beta assets are sometimes considered "defensive" because they can act as a hedge against broader market declines.

- **Sharpe Ratio:** A calculation of the excess return (return above a risk-free rate, typically three-month U.S. Treasury Bills) per unit of risk (usually represented by standard deviation). A higher Sharpe Ratio indicates better risk-adjusted performance.

- **Treynor Ratio:** A calculation similar to the Sharpe Ratio, that also considers excess return, but it uses beta as a measure of risk instead of standard deviation. Beta reflects the sensitivity of an investment to overall market movements.

- **Sortino Ratio:** A measure used to evaluate an investment's return relative to its downside risk. It is an extension of the Sharpe ratio, which only considers the total risk (both upside and downside), whereas the Sortino ratio focuses solely on the downside risk. The Sortino ratio was introduced to address the criticism that the Sharpe ratio may penalize investments for upside volatility, even if it is desirable.

- **Jensen's Alpha:** A measure to assess an investment's performance by comparing its actual return to the expected return based on its beta. A positive alpha means the investment outperformed the predicted return, while a negative alpha means it underperformed.

- **Information Ratio:** A measure of the ability of a portfolio manager to generate returns above a benchmark index, considering the active risk taken. It evaluates the manager's skill in selecting securities or assets.

Risk-adjusted rates of return provide a more comprehensive perspective on an investment manager's performance, but they do not necessarily illuminate qualitative factors of an investment process that are essential to understand what drives a particular strategy.

FIRST PRINCIPLES AND SIMPLE RULES

The Benefits of Observing Financial Behavior Over Multiple Market Cycles

Simple Rules

I like to keep things simple. I can summarize my perspective and lessons as follows:

- Rule number one: *Think independently and trust your judgment. If you do not understand a strategy, avoid it.*
- Rule number two: *History is a solid guide to the future.*
- Rule number three: *Establish a disciplined framework of continuous review for your decisions and follow your own rules for investing.*
- Rule number four: *Do not violate your rules or act based on emotional responses.*

The first principle is that stocks have provided the opportunity to preserve purchasing power over time but have been volatile, and they have and will test investors' resolve. Studies have documented the tendency of investors to sell after significant stock market declines and then buy back their positions after it has begun to recover. Unsurprisingly, this has led to returns of less than the market average for individual investors. Establishing the resolve to execute a long-term strategy during periods of perhaps terrifying stock market declines is what is necessary to increase the probability that one can achieve investment objectives.

The second principle is that it is extremely difficult to exit stock allocations successfully and persistently before declines and to reestablish them before the market recovers. Long-term investors need not engage in stock market timing if history is a guide, which I firmly believe that it is.

All investors should have a plan within which they can judge their progress. As the boxer Mike Tyson quipped, "Everyone has a plan 'till they get punched in the mouth." Plans should anticipate outcomes with varying probabilities and should include the assumption that just because patterns of financial markets may be within certain parameters most of the time, they still may deviate dramatically below or above those of the past. Risk is palpable when the investor "gets punched in the mouth." But like so much in life we may worry about many things that never occur, but to avoid all risks has its own highly certain probability, which may not be attractive.

As time passes it is easy to lose sight of the tests that the stock market has presented. We witnessed equity market irrational exuberance in the late 1990s as well as fear after the Dot Com bubble, five years of recovery from October 2002 until October 2007, then the Great Financial Crisis that began in late 2007, and then the eventual recovery to historically elevated levels of stock market value through 2021. The stock market decline in 2022 was followed by a partial recovery through December 2023. Investors weathered two approximately 50% declines between March 2000 and October 2002. When one hundred goes to fifty, getting back to one hundred requires a 100% increase. The simple math can induce fear in the most seasoned investor, but those who remain resolute and execute their long-term strategies are rewarded. Indeed, those who followed their strategies to maintain allocations to stock, and added to them in the depths of the decline, enjoyed an amplified recovery. Such additions were made with the proceeds of fixed-income securities that did not decline and sometimes increased during the stock market declines. This is called rebalancing the portfolio. While rebalancing strategy allocations may seem too simplistic, it has worked. We found that rebalancing was usually indicated after at least a 20% stock market decline. Of course, the future may differ from the past, but financial behavior reflects human reactions that are unlikely to change over time.

It is those reactions upon which our approach derives its recommendations. Raw fear and then greed are most visible during stock market declines, and sometimes during rapid recoveries that occur in brief time periods. There is no question that one's resolve about investing for the long term will be tested, with significant doubt during market declines. It is the fear and greed extremes that can help us understand our own reactions to downturns in the stock market. I should note that during such extreme periods, the financial media have been overflowing with those who have reasons to be fearful about the future.

Friends have expressed their lack of understanding about investing and would like to bring order to the often chaotic and random messages of financial markets. How do we confront and reconcile something that we do not understand? History and our everyday life experiences provide guidance for us to manage our reactions to inevitable uncertainty and to plan for the unknown.

We need to understand the opportunities and risks we have in life, as well as our finances, and to acknowledge our emotional biases when making any decisions. We observe rules that help us avoid harm in our daily lives. Look both ways at a stop sign before proceeding, be courteous, and other conventions and habits that guide us and our relationship with others. The same should be true when we consider the value of our financial assets. Naturally, we want to avoid any decisions that we may regret. We can benefit from some well-defined guardrails and perspectives by avoiding decisions driven by our emotions more than our logic. Conventional advice is to avoid important decisions when in a heightened emotional state, which to me is exceptional advice.

Inevitably, our investment decisions require an assessment of probabilities over various periods of time. One's risk tolerance can be defined as the level below which one will not tolerate further loss of dollar amounts, below a starting value, that a portfolio may experience 95% of the time. The other 5% of the time events occur like the Great Financial Crisis when the stock market declined by nearly 60% from its peak in late 2007, until its bottom in early March 2009. How should we respond if the 5% probability occurs, either positively or negatively? Investors with resolve endured the terrifying and protracted decline in stock prices but enjoyed the recovery that more than made up for the unrealized losses. Those who exited their stock allocations faced an exceedingly difficult decision after the stock market advanced significantly and swiftly, in addition to incurring tax liabilities for any of their realized net gains.

The framework within which we can assess probable outcomes given our risk and return preferences is not perfect, but in my experience, has served well during several major financial market declines.

The framework to which I refer should be available from your current investment advisor and projects probable return above and below your current asset value, within six-month intervals. Why six months? Because while we might think that we are long-term investors looking at time horizons of multiple years, we are influenced by much shorter-term outcomes. Research by the Nobel Prize-winning psychologist Daniel Kahneman provides an encouraging and utilitarian framework. Kahneman proposed Prospect Theory as a discipline to determine risk preferences. It suggests that people treat gains differently than losses in two respects. Individuals make choices to minimize losses more than they gamble for possible gains, and when faced with two negative prospects, 92% of respondents chose the option with a lower expected value to avoid losses. In short, Prospect Theory holds that losses hurt more than gains feel good. Of course, the dilemma is that risk assumption is essential to generate meaningful gains.

A carefully constructed structure of probability protocol can help to avoid emotional responses, like selling all stocks after a major decline in value, which many did in early 2009 just before the stock market recovered and advanced for over ten years. The process accommodates and quantifies the concept of randomness, which is a fact of life. It calculates multiple scenarios to define losses that can be tolerated, and losses that are most likely to occur. The fact is that stock values can decline to zero, so the maximum loss can be total. We cannot plan for Armageddon and should not fear planning for the most probable outcomes. Well, we could plan for Armageddon, but even holding cash, gold or diamonds might not be what we need most in a meltdown of the financial markets, and the related chaos it would cause. In the meantime, our return on capital would be no better than the yield that we might earn on cash equivalents like savings accounts or money market funds.

The Importance of Disciplined Review and the Potential Cost of Inertia

A particularly important lesson that I learned in my career is that most people do not want to subject their investment decisions to scrutiny and that inertia about their money takes over. Also, many do not acknowledge their concerns about their investments. Change is difficult. They rarely if ever admit to mistakes with their decisions. We have all heard the stories about their successes. As an investment advisor when I meet people, they are frequently very defensive about their investment plan, even though I never raise the subject, as to me it would be an intrusive inquiry. They assume that I am like most in the industry and would try to persuade them to engage me to manage their account. I was selective about accepting clients, so unless someone asked specifically about my advice, I never raised the subject. I did not accept those as clients who thought that I or anyone else could successfully time exposure to the stock market. A conventional statement from most people is that they are fine with their investment program, whether they have objectively evaluated it or not.

The discipline of a review framework is essential to execute a successful long-term investment plan. If you review your account regularly you are ahead of the game. No, I do not mean that one should check their portfolio daily, because the markets are volatile and tend to overreact to news that may have only a transitory impact on fundamental values, upon which long-term strategies are based. Review your investments at least quarterly, especially when you know that your portfolio value has declined. Ask the simple questions, and the answers usually reveal themselves. It is easy to set aside difficult decisions, or even sometimes to confront the reality of a disappointing interval in the stock market, but remain resolute in your periodic review and maintain the perspective that you adopted when establishing your strategy and asset allocation policy targets and limits.

Of course, one could sell short and profit from declining stock prices. The only problem with shorting stocks is that there is unlimited risk if the stock appreciates, and the most that one could earn is the difference between the price at which the stock was sold, short and zero.

Time is not on your side if you have sold stocks short, and it is if you hold stocks for the long term. The fact is that the S&P 500 Composite Stock Price Index, which was started in 1926, has produced an after-inflation annualized rate of return of 7.0% with dividends reinvested before any taxes and 3.2% without reinvesting dividends. A 3.2% rate of return after inflation may not seem attractive, but over only ten years $10,000 will increase to $13,702, which means that your purchasing power will increase by 37%, depending on the tax rate that will reduce the return. The more frequently quoted annualized rate of return, before adjusting for inflation and taxes, has been 10.1% with dividends reinvested, and 6.2% without reinvesting dividends. Of course, if the assets are held in a qualified retirement account for ten years and earn the average historical rate in the S&P 500, they will accumulate at 6.2% in ten years and be worth $18,249 or produce 82% more purchasing power.

It is important to note that the nine years ended June 30, 2009, recorded an annualized nominal, before inflation *loss* of 3.2% with dividends reinvested, and 4.9% without dividends reinvested. The Dot Com bubble burst in March 2000. This meant that one dollar lost 32% of its value with dividends reinvested in that nine years, if invested in the S&P 500 in a tax-free retirement account. Those who remained invested in stocks reaped the rewards of recovered stock prices. The main reason for the return to those holding stocks for the long term is that corporations on balance produced increasing earnings and value.

Fees Matter, Especially as Asset Values Grow

Investment costs are a crucial element of any investment program and can be controlled. How much more time or work does it take to manage a million-dollar portfolio than a $500,000 portfolio? Yet the fee for the million-dollar portfolio is typically twice that of the $500,000 portfolio. Like other aspects of our lives, such as online shopping and overnight or same-day delivery of goods, access to information in every aspect of our lives has delivered efficiency that was previously hard to imagine. How many of us knew that we needed rapid home delivery of all manner of goods until Amazon started in the mid-1990s? Of course, its competitors followed with their own online shopping facilities, and its impact on brick-and-mortar stores has been profound, ultimately saving consumers billions of dollars in the aggregate. How many of us knew that we needed mobile devices before the iPhone was introduced in 2007? The most successful products or services have created their own demand, and most never knew that they needed them until they were readily available. I believe that the same will be true for those who believe that they should engage investment advisors to provide service for fees, that most do not understand, and that are conventionally based on the size of the assets managed; not the actual time, value, or insight delivered by the manager. The actual cost of such professional advice can be significantly reduced, or even eliminated, by the individual investor who takes control of their own investment program.

While many everyday investors have adopted the more accessible investment vehicles, the traditional investment advisory model is attractive to many who may not fully understand the cost they pay in return for perceived comfort. Efficiency will likely continue to improve, but unlike the period just before and during the Dot Com Boom of the late 1990s to early 2000s, when many heralded the "New Economy," economic behavior and decisions have not changed, because the fundamental principles of capitalism and investing have not changed. Our collective behavior has not changed.

Everybody wants to reduce uncertainty and increase their comfort level, but like any other actual or perceived insurance against undesirable outcomes, there is a cost. We should all understand the costs because they reduce one's investment return. The value of advice can be subjective, and it is always the client who determines such value. The world of institutional investing that I participated in for my career was judged on actual net performance, not subjective opinions of a program's effectiveness, or the likeability of its investment advisors. I like to keep things simple and present my review of financial markets and the investment process for perspective, and for those ready to take control of their investment programs and their financial futures. And, to do so with confidence, joy, and peace of mind.

Summary

- The first principle is that stocks have provided the opportunity to preserve purchasing power over time but have been volatile and test investors' resolve.
- The second principle is that it is extremely difficult to exit stock allocations successfully, and persistently, before declines and to reestablish them before the market recovers.
- Rules matter. All investors should have a plan within which they can judge their progress. Do not let inertia overcome the necessity of disciplined reviews.
- Corporations on balance have produced increasing earnings and enterprise value for shareholders, which is the reason to own stocks.
- Investment management fees matter.

INVEST FEARLESSLY

Embrace Investment Opportunity:
You are Your Own Chief Investment Officer

Time Preference and Investor Mindset

It is essential to determine your time preference. Would you rather spend income and assets, or invest them for the future? Of course, most people will balance the time preference of their perceived current needs against their expected needs. It may mean that we sacrifice certain expenditures in the present, which is an integral part of the discipline necessary to accumulate funds for the future. Investing is based on the idea that we have decided to save, and that the investment will generate a return for ourselves and perhaps others, who either borrow it or deploy our capital in equity in a business. Individuals should design and execute a disciplined and continuous structure to plan and implement efficient investment programs—and save a valuable amount of their fee and commission money otherwise paid to professional investment firms.

If there were no inflation and the dollar maintained its purchasing power, investing with the risk of loss would not be necessary, except to potentially enhance your savings. If bank savings accounts offered interest rates that were available over the long term and were at, or above, the rate of inflation after taxes, one should allocate savings to them if one is risk averse. To date, savings accounts have not offered such rates. Many opt for the comfort of an insured savings account, but that insurance comes at a significant cost. The opportunity to generate higher rates of return requires the saver to assume the risk of loss. Your advisor should be able to provide you with an objective measure of your prospective portfolio risk, and if they have not done so, you should request a review of this crucial factor.

Recent history has demonstrated that just playing it safe in bank savings accounts has carried a significant cost in terms of their money's purchasing power, even in a low-inflation environment. On a long-term basis, including the time necessary to accumulate sufficient funds for retirement, the interest paid by banks after taxes and inflation has been, and is likely to continue to be, insufficient to maintain the purchasing power of your money. Yes, your savings account balance may never decline, but it will, if history is a guide, grow too slowly relative to your needs in the future with any inflation at all. Even at 2% annual inflation, the purchasing power of the dollar will decline to eighty-two cents over ten years.

The Consumer Price Index calculated by the U.S. Bureau of Labor Statistics reported that it would take $1.31 in August 2023 to purchase $1.00 of goods or services ten years earlier. During the same time, one dollar invested in the S&P 500 Index on August 1, 2013, with dividends reinvested and held with no changes, returned 10.3% a year including the decline in 2022, thus a dollar invested in the S&P 500 Index would increase by $1.67 to $2.67.

The fact is that even the probably understated rate of Consumer Price Inflation calculated by the government shows the pernicious impact of inflation that we all experience and underscores the importance of investing to preserve purchasing power. Over longer periods, the impact of inflation is starker, even at seemingly benign rates of 2%.

Aside from the important need to identify investment objectives, time horizon, and risk tolerance, investors need to adopt a mindset that supports accepting the risks. Rather than accept the conventional view that investing is complex and that financial markets are chaotic, so individuals should just leave their investment decisions to professionals, I believe that once you understand the basic principles of investing you can apply them to your benefit in the most efficient way possible. Think of this knowledge and discipline as a tool for paying yourself, not an advisor.

This chapter presents a course of action for investors that must be predicated on understanding stock market behavior over the long term. How do we determine our tolerance for investment risk before it is exceeded? Investment advisory services often describe varying investment risk profiles by labeling strategies with terms such as capital preservation, conservative, income-oriented, moderate growth, growth, or aggressive growth for example. Those terms and others like them are subjective, and one person's growth strategy may differ substantially from another's. Fitting a client's strategy into broad categories and then populating a portfolio with funds or securities intended to comport with those categories, with essentially blanket recommendations for asset allocation and security, or fund selection, across similar client objectives is unlikely to deliver confidence during a significant stock market decline.

In his acclaimed and bestselling book *Thinking, Fast and Slow*, Daniel Kahneman found that people tend not to have foresight about the risks in their lives and investments and, unsurprisingly, react to gains and losses. It describes the dichotomy between thinking fast, or instinctively and emotionally, and thinking more slowly or more deliberatively, without emotion. The research also found that people are in general 2.5 times more concerned about losses than they are about gains. It is for this reason that the investor must determine the maximum market value decline that one can endure.

Friends have expressed their lack of understanding of investing and would like to bring order to the often chaotic and random messages of financial markets. How do we confront and reconcile something that we do not understand? I believe that history provides guidance for us to manage our reactions to inevitable uncertainty and to plan for the unknown. Kahneman's book describes how we view decisions, and what is especially striking is that his work concludes that we have more risk in our lives than we may see clearly or even accept. How can we identify the risks and prepare for them? You can invest independently without engaging professional guidance. If you seek professional advice on your investment planning, you can engage as an investment advisor on an asset-based fee basis or, as a bridge, engage a coach for a fixed fee to help you get started on an enduring investment program and save ongoing fees. My new-era firm addresses this challenge objectively and definitively, within a range of probable outcomes based on specific investor preferences in dollar terms. Your current advisor may have access to programs that calculate your preferences for return and tolerance for risk, so you should ask them to assist you. The structural advantage of a continuous review and inquiry process within a clear framework of fundamental principles has the potential to anticipate, and then respond, to a negative change in a measured way, with the perspective of a strategy based on probabilities. This process helps to increase the probability of the desired outcome.

I encourage you to embrace the challenges of investing with the confidence that a broad perspective can deliver. Investing need not be a mystery.

Your Customized Return Appetite and Risk Tolerance

Investors are typically asked to characterize their investment appetite for return, and tolerance for risk, with well-meaning but subjective terms that fall short when assessing probable returns or losses in dollars and cents. We are talking about real money, not a hypothetical exercise and one should have as high a confidence level as possible about outcomes in an uncertain world. I advocate a tangible range of probabilities in dollar terms around one's current asset value. One person's growth could well be another person's conservative posture. A team of academics performed an assessment of subjective terms to define preferences and found that 52% of twenty- to twenty-nine-year-olds are not *aggressive,* and 53% of —seventy- to seventy-nine-year-olds are not *conservative!"* This is exactly the opposite of what one would expect.

The key to eliminating anxiety about investing is to objectively determine risk tolerance and return appetite. Our approach is to determine a long-term investor's appetite for return, and tolerance for risk, in dollar terms over a six-month period. The reason for six months is that it is a time period to which most can relate. If actual experience remains within the probability range, which is calculated at 95%, the confidence investors have is increased to stay with their long-term plan. One can also stress test one's portfolio in different financial market scenarios, including major events like the Great Financial Crises, rising interest rates, rising price inflation, or recessions, for example. This analysis allows one to calibrate their specific portfolio holdings more confidently and to adhere to a long-term strategy.

Our process begins with questions to determine one's risk and return preferences based on Prospect Theory and starts with stating one's financial goals and proceeds to financial sentiment, such as one's positive, neutral, or negative view of financial markets and the level of confidence that one has in their financial future. Prospect Theory is where individuals choose which probability of gain and loss they prefer. For example, would a loss of a specific dollar amount, and gain in terms of dollars below and above your present portfolio value, be acceptable within the 95% probability range over six months? If that is not acceptable, reduce the probable loss and gain until an acceptable level of risk and return is likely. The questions are iterative and depend upon previous answers and preferences. The iterative questions begin with one's current asset value and proceed to the question about how one might feel about a particular decline in value compared to a hypothetical increase in value, versus a certain outcome relative to the current value. If we reduce risk enough, we can derive a certain outcome, but that forecloses the opportunity to improve value very much. The next four questions proceed by narrowing risk and return preferences relative to certain outcomes. The answers are then used to calculate a risk score that defines the 95% range of probable returns in dollar terms, above and below the current asset value. Respondents are also asked if they would sell their assets if they reached the downside limit, or if they would stay invested in anticipation of recovery. The respondent's answer is designed to reveal their visceral reaction to a loss. If it is high, there is too much risk in the portfolio, and it must be reduced at the expense of a lower potential return. This process requires specialized calculators or applications that advisors should have available.

It is natural for those unfamiliar with mathematical probability calculations to adopt the conventionally recommended investment structures and to doubt the validity of projections. Projections present a framework against which to gauge progress in the often seemingly groundless behavior of financial markets. It is that framework that helps us to understand ourselves and our relationship to our money. And . . . it has worked.

We cannot know the outcome of an investment program with the certainty that we probably want, but we can embrace the challenge of investing with a clear framework for assessing risk, intentions, and policies, and we can control the costs. It is vital for the investor to determine a tolerance for investment risk before it is exceeded. If you exceed your tolerance for risk, it may lead to decisions based on fear of further declines in value. Stock market history has rewarded those who remained resolute but is unforgiving to those who allow emotions to rule their decisions. That is either the emotion of fear or greed.

Simple but Not Simplistic Advice

We have seen that one can benefit by investing in stocks for the long term, and it is excellent advice. It is simple, but not simplistic advice. The problem that some people have with benefiting from this simple advice is that stock market volatility leads to shorter-term thinking and then often to emotional responses that defeat the "stocks for the long term" strategy. The benefits of long-term investing and dollar cost averaging one's purchases have been significant and have delivered financial security to many people. Dollar-cost averaging means investing the same amount of money in a security at regular intervals over time, regardless of price. The investor will have exposure to the security as prices decline and increase, thereby buying more shares when the price is lower than when it is higher. It is a good discipline for long-term investors who add fresh cash to their portfolios.

While it may be enticing to engage in shorter-term strategies or stock picking, one should calibrate such activity proportionately in a total portfolio context, so as not to defeat the overall strategy of owning stocks if the outcome of trading is unprofitable. The concentration of positions can be extremely rewarding, and the automatic diversification of favored positions may not be optimal depending upon the investor's conviction in and knowledge about the company. Investors with concentrated positions may want to perform scenario analyses to assess their prospective conviction, given the potentially extreme price fluctuation and its impact on those shares of the total portfolio.

Trust your judgment and common sense, take responsibility, and be your own most trusted advisor. No one will ride to your rescue. Well, that is arguably not true as the Federal Reserve policy has been supportive of financial markets by providing increased amounts of liquidity through its Open Market operations, which is a euphemistic way of saying that it prints money out of thin air when it deems it necessary. We saw this in action after the Covid scare in February 2020, and again in March 2023 when Silicon Valley Bank failed. Fed actions have provided liquidity and essentially support after stock market declines, typically to support the full employment mandate that Congress has ordered.

The fact is that investing and access to efficient and low-cost investment vehicles have changed dramatically in the past twenty years, which has made investing for everyday people easier than ever. Access to in-depth information is also easier. Think about it. We may do several searches before buying regular personal, household items, or services, and even watch videos of product or service reviews, so why not spend the same energy and do the same comparison shopping when structuring an investment program strategy or engaging an advisor who will charge you fees every day?

The frequent advertisements from established mutual funds and other investment advisory firms are hard to ignore. They follow us around in our Internet use and are ubiquitous during televised sports events. Sure, attractive videos of people having fun with the money that their advisor apparently made for them may be enticing, but the reality is that the value added by advisors over a diversified portfolio managed by you may not be so clear. Statements like "My advisor did a great job for me because my portfolio is up" are not uncommon, but when asked how their performance compares to an unmanaged index composite, they are often silent or more often dismissive. The fact that the firms doing such advertising are enormous with hundreds of billions or trillions of dollars under advisement, and whose brands are ubiquitous, may well persuade prospective clients that that firm is skillful when managing your portfolios, so please ask and understand how they add value for you. The only reason to pay fees is for value-added. **A bull market should never be confused with brilliance.** The last chapter will go into detail on how to evaluate an advisor.

Successful investing in my opinion requires a realistic and common-sense approach to our decisions regarding our investments but also to our everyday lives. Why everyday life? Because we all have our own rules, habits, and routines for avoiding the usual risks in our lives. We probably know that when we violate our own rules the outcome can be harmful to our well-being. Following rules with our investing is essential to reaching our goals and doing so with confidence. Financial markets certainly appear to be chaotic, but the fundamentals that ultimately drive financial behavior expressed in market pricing are not. Understand basic principles and adhere to your own framework for decisions about investing that will permit you to have more confidence about an uncertain future.

History does not exactly repeat itself, but it rhymes and will continue to test investor resolve

During my career, we had a few panics that may have faded from memory. One of the more dramatic times was the Crash of 1987. Many investors today did not experience this steep decline, but it was a stark lesson. It caused calamity in markets and was triggered by a then newer strategy of "portfolio insurance," using options and futures that failed to work as expected, to preserve value during a market decline. That 32% decline lasted for two months and stock markets recovered gradually. The subsequent recovery was enjoyed by those who did not liquidate their positions in the tumult of the decline. More recently, the two months of decline in the S&P 500 in February and March 2020 was -20.5%, but it recovered the loss by August of 2020.

The mid-1990s witnessed the rise in the popularity of relatively few mega-capitalized company stocks and unusually high multi-year mid-teens percentage returns that gave investors more confidence that it would continue to generate much higher than historical rates of return. Such elevated expectations coincided with the rise of the Internet and web-based companies that rushed their embryonic offerings to the public stock markets in what was a near frenzy, where fundamental factors were cast aside except for the distant potential growth of revenues. That stock market advance peaked in March 2000 and has been characterized as the Dot-Com Bubble. The stock market declined 50.5% until October 2002, as many fledging companies failed, and their stock was worthless. Investor behavior can go to extremes, that in hindsight look plainly irrational while the savvier investors probably did not participate in the final stages of that frenzy. There is a saying in finance that the market can remain irrational longer than some can remain solvent. In other words, investors must be prepared to be resolute with their holdings provided that fundamental factors are intact. The S&P 500 Index bottomed out in October 2002, and in October 2007 it recovered to its Dot-Com peak level.

The S&P 500 peaked in October 2007, and the Great Financial Crisis began in the spring of 2008 when Bear Stearns was near insolvency and was purchased by J.P. Morgan. Although there was temporary relief in financial markets after that purchase, and the Fed stood by with minor changes in its policy, the worst was still in front of us as Lehman Brothers failed in September 2008 and the financial and banking system nearly stopped functioning. From its high in October 2007 until its bottom in March 2009, the S&P 500 Index declined 57.7%. For more perspective, for those who held stocks from the Dot-Com peak until the eventual bottom in March 2009, the S&P 500 was down 47.5% and its annualized rate of return without dividends was -6.9%, but subsequent advances recovered all the decline.

Lines on a graph may not convey the magnitude of stock market volatility, so I present the S&P 500 Index levels and percentage changes for clarity. Those who remained resolute after the Great Financial Crisis enjoyed an increase in the S&P 500 Index from 676, the bottom on March 9, 2009, to 3,386 on February 19, 2020—a 400% increase until the Covid pandemic appeared. Covid elevated uncertainty, and the S&P 500 declined from 3,386 on February 19, 2020, to 2,237 on March 23, 2020, or 34%. A 34% decline in a month tested investor resolve. The next S&P 500 Index peak occurred on December 29, 2021, at 4,793, a 114% increase from the March 2020 low, and a 609% increase from the March 2009 low.

In 2022 the S&P 500 declined, and bonds also declined in price such that the total return in 2022 for the S&P 500 was -18.1% and bonds, as measured by the popular Bloomberg U.S. Aggregate Bond Index, were down 13.0%. The Bloomberg U.S. Aggregate Bond Index is a proxy for investment-grade domestic bonds and includes government as well as corporate issues. It is generally regarded as a reliable benchmark. Lehman Brothers created the index in the early 1970s, and it was ultimately sponsored by the Bloomberg organization.

Can You Time our Exposure to the Stock Market?

In just the past twenty-three years, we have seen two more than 50% declines in the S&P 500 with a surging stock market advance until late December 2021. Only those who participated in equities and endured the declines benefited from the risk. Why not just avoid the declines and get in before the advances? Because the probability of correctly timing exposure to the stock market is extremely low. The studies that we did at my former firm revealed that from 1961 to 2017, if one missed just 4.2% of the months of S&P 500 advance, their annualized return would have been the same as the return of 3-month U.S. Treasury Bills. One dollar invested in the S&P 500 would have grown to $182.92, a 9.9% annualized rate of return, and one dollar in U.S. Treasury Bills to $14.42, a 5% per annum return– but only to $14.26 if one missed the best twenty-eight months of the stock market. Another way of stating these facts is to observe that the S&P 500 did nothing relative to an investment in no-risk 3-month U.S. Treasury Bills for 95.8% of the time. Not a prediction, but a mathematical fact that is challenged daily by the popular financial media outlets, that present commentators who make predictions about stock market direction and behavior daily for short-term intervals, like next week, month, or year. To my knowledge, no one has ever presented evidence that their short-term predictions were accurate consistently.

Stock market history is more than just math as described in the market timing example described above, but it is powerful math indeed. In my decades of analyzing investment managers, I found only a few people with the acumen to correctly and persistently time their exposure to the stock market, and they typically attracted enough money in their strategy after a few years or less to close to new investors. Such skill is exceedingly rare. It is amusing that the financial media highlights strategists almost daily who opine about their very short-term view of stock market direction and rarely, if ever, disclose the record of the strategist. One outlet regularly interviewed a manager who expressed a persistently negative view of the stock market for a decade after the market began its recovery from the 2007 to 2009 decline. The manager was always articulate and apparently had a firm grasp of the factors important at that moment but was persistently wrong—and unaccountable. The major financial media outlet interviews this individual regularly on its broadcasts, but I have never heard them provide any disclaimer of the individual's record of predictions. Not once did the media outlet ask the individual to discuss his actual performance. Ironically, it is probably because the commentator managed a private placement hedge fund and is prohibited from discussing performance publicly. The world is filled with irony and in this case, there was zero transparency due to SEC regulations. Only accredited investors and qualified purchasers, which are regulatory terms described in the chapter on investment choices for those with significant liquid assets, are permitted to have access to private fund performance data and offering memoranda.

Summary

- You are your own chief investment officer.
- Probable investment risk can be assessed and managed.
- The importance of rules.
- Two declines of approximately 50% have occurred twice between mid-1999 and mid-2009, leading to a decade of lost value for stock investors. Stock market declines of a similar magnitude can certainly occur again.
- Emotional resilience is essential for stock investors whether using a wealth manager or investing independently.
- The technical measures of risk-adjusted rates of return are not generally relevant for individual investors investing in a broad index of publicly traded stocks.
- Timing exposure to the stock market has a very low probability of consistent success and presents a risk that long-term investors need not bear.
- Be cautious of stock market advice when emotions may be elevated by either a steep decline or an increase in stock prices.

DO IT YOURSELF

AN INDIVIDUAL CAN INVEST with no outside advice if they understand what to expect from their portfolio as markets fluctuate. One can invest in securities with no minimum and with no fees in index funds. The key is to start.

The ratio of stock to bonds in typical portfolios is usually 60%, or 70% in stocks and 40% to 30% in bonds. Over time, but not necessarily annually, these allocation ratios have worked. When the stock market has declined bonds, until 2022, typically advanced in price or stayed relatively stable and reduced volatility, as well as being a source of funds to rebalance strategy allocations in stocks. Lower allocations to equity securities means lower risk of decline. These allocations imply different volatility as described below on the importance of asset allocation. The key is to maintain resolve when the market declines and to rebalance the portfolio to take advantage of stocks that are on sale after stock market declines. There is no guarantee that stocks will not go to zero value, so calibrate your equity exposure carefully. To say that there is a non-zero chance that stocks can go to zero value is true, but unlikely. As mentioned earlier, more things can happen than will happen, but to plan for the worst is likely to impair opportunity materially. Diversification is the primary way to manage risk.

Today individuals have access to cost-free services at large mutual fund companies that can assist in the planning and implementation of their assets. The only fees that one should expect to pay are those charged by the ETF of the mutual fund selected.

Common stocks have offered the most practical and liquid means to preserve purchasing power after inflation and taxes. This principle is true and well-accepted based on at least the last hundred years of quality data. Will it change in the future? Anything can happen, but the fact that corporate stock ownership of a broad group of entities reflects rational financial behavior on a long-term basis, if not necessarily in the short term when it can be quite volatile. Companies manage their assets for shareholders and are rewarded for doing so successfully. While the companies are held to a high standard of accountability, and not just legally, free market forces determine the value of the shares in their companies in the equity market. We can all remember those formerly dominant companies that have faded or failed, especially since the Internet began in the 1990s. New companies have become dominant by providing valuable goods and services that did not exist in 2000 or later. Those that have reinvented themselves have also thrived. New and successfully evolved companies are the ones that have driven the return of stock indices, such as the S&P 500.

Independent thinking may sound obvious, but when regaled by promotional advertisements and solicitations it may be more difficult to maintain independence than we prefer. After all, the large and established firms making such overtures must be doing something right for their customers. Or are they? I am fully cognizant that many, if not most, people engage registered investment advisors for the comfort that they perceive they will have. The pitch is something like: "Do not worry just leave all your important investment decisions to us, we are professionals." Another lesson is that, as previously mentioned, very few advisors persistently perform better than broad equity market indices, yet they are paid handsomely for taking that risk with client assets. My perspective challenges conventional practices in the investment advisory industry that are bound by what I believe are outdated fee arrangements that in many, if not most situations cost clients more than the value they add. Unfortunately, too many investment advisors do not provide the transparency necessary for clients to readily see how much value they add after their fees and trust that clients do not ask the obvious, but important questions.

A particularly important lesson that I learned is that most people do not want to subject their investment decisions to scrutiny and that inertia about their money takes over. Also, many do not acknowledge their concerns about their investments. The discipline of a review framework is essential to execute a successful long-term investment plan. If you review your account regularly you are ahead of the game. No, I do not mean that one should check their portfolio daily, because the markets are volatile and tend to overreact to news that may have only a transitory impact on fundamental values upon which long-term strategies are based. Review your investments at least quarterly, especially when you know that your portfolio value has declined. Ask the simple questions, and the answers usually reveal themselves. It is easy to set aside tough decisions, or even sometimes to confront the reality of a disappointing interval in the stock market but remain resolute in your periodic review and maintain the perspective that you reviewed when establishing your strategy and asset allocation policy targets and limits. You will have a structural advantage if you regularly and objectively review your portfolio.

The Importance of Asset Allocation

Asset allocation is the most crucial decision one can make in investment planning. A landmark study found that asset allocation accounted for 91.5% of portfolio returns. Only 8.5% of portfolio returns could be attributed to the selection of specific securities. (Source: Brinson, Singer, and Beebower, "Determinants of Portfolio Performance II: An Update," *Financial Analysts Journal*, May/June 1991.)

Two basic approaches to asset allocation are strategic and tactical. Without question, a strategic approach is less risky than a tactical approach, in my opinion. Strategic refers to a long-term time horizon and defines the percentage allocations of each asset class. It requires adjustments back to those stipulated levels when they change due to market fluctuation, commonly referred to as rebalancing. Rebalancing may appear to be simplistic, but it captures the tendency of returns to return to their average or mean levels. It reduces the asset class that outperforms the others in the portfolio and increases the allocation to those that relatively underperform. In other words, it buys assets that have gotten less expensive and sells those that have maintained or increased in value. This strategy has worked well at increments of 20% change. For example, if an equity allocation declines from 70% of the total to 56% of the portfolio, a 20% decline, one would restore the allocation to 70% with proceeds from the relatively outperforming categories, usually bonds. Holding cash may feel good, but it presents a long-term opportunity cost. Naturally, the equity market has declined more than 20% in the past and is likely to do so again, but the advantage of rebalancing is that if performed with discipline it has shown to be effective. The probability of timing exposure to the equity market successfully is very low, and rebalancing sidesteps the risk of unsuccessful timing.

Tactical asset allocation attempts to adjust asset category commitments to stocks and bonds based on forecasts of market direction and/or on the relative valuation of portfolio constituents or potential constituents. The practice may deliver acceptable outcomes, but it presents risks not present with strategic investing in equities. Given the clear expectation that the tactical approach assumes successful market timing, it is not one with a high probability of success.

It is important to note that an asset class or category is defined by its structural sources of return. Stocks pay dividends and represent a call on the assets and earning power of an enterprise, and bonds pay a stated coupon interest and mature at their par value, for example. Commodities are priced as a function of supply and demand, as there is no other return to owning them and there may be a cost, such as the custody and insurance costs of owning gold bullion, for example. The higher price of a commodity usually drives more production and increases the supply of that commodity. Therefore, the price self-regulates relative to additional supply. Real estate derives its return from income, utility, and potentially scarcity of supply relative to demand. The chapter on investment choices explains in more detail the diverse types of investments that one might select.

The asset allocation planning approach typically uses asset class benchmarks for basically similar securities, usually indices or other portfolio constituent types to model or project expected returns, and the variability of those returns that is expressed in terms of standard deviation. Our approach refines the process and uses individual portfolio constituents rather than indices of groups of securities, such as the S&P 500. Standard deviation is a measure of how values deviate above and below the average of the data series, or in this case security prices. The annual standard deviation of the

S&P 500 is approximately 15%, and its long-term average rate of return has been approximately 10% with dividends reinvested and no tax, which is the case in qualified retirement funds like IRAs or 401k plans. One standard deviation occurs about 68% of the time, and two standard deviations occur about 95% of the time. This implies that the return may be plus 25% or minus 5%, 68% of the years, and between plus 35% or minus 20%, 95% of the time. The other 5% of the time implies that returns could be higher than 35% or lower than minus 20%. Of course, there can be no guarantee that these limits will persist.

Harry Markowitz, an American Nobel prize-winning economist, who recently passed away, is best known for his development of Modern Portfolio Theory (MPT). MPT is a framework that helps investors optimize their portfolios by balancing risk and return. MPT has been used widely in institutional investing successfully for many years and there is no reason to expect its utility to change. Perhaps counterintuitively, the math shows that portfolio constituents that have low correlations to each other can enhance returns as values deviate from each other at the same time. There is a benefit to having a low correlation of those constituents that zig when the others zag, provided that the constituents produce acceptable longer-term returns.

Key concepts of Modern Portfolio Theory include:

- Diversification: Holding a variety of assets that are not perfectly correlated can potentially reduce the impact of inferior performance in any single investment.
- Efficient Frontier: The efficient frontier is usually expressed as a graph that displays the combinations of assets that provide the highest expected return for a given level of risk, or the lowest risk for a given level of expected return.

- Risk and Return: MPT seeks to help investors optimize the balance between risk and return based on their individual preferences.
- Correlation and Covariance: MPT emphasizes the importance of considering not only the individual risks and returns of assets but also their correlations and covariances. Correlations measure how assets move in relation to each other, and covariances capture the joint variability of asset returns. These measures help in understanding how assets interact within a portfolio and are integral to our process.
- Optimal Portfolio Allocation: MPT involves using mathematical modeling to determine the optimal allocation of assets in a portfolio. Typically, the calculations are complex and consider many combinations of the different assets that the investor considers for inclusion in the portfolio. The goal is to maximize the expected return for a given level of risk or minimize the risk for a given level of expected return.
- Risk-Free Asset: Risk-free assets such as short-term U.S. Treasury Bills serve as the foundation for constructing portfolios and measuring their relative risk. The goal is to create portfolios that have optimal risk and return prospects.

Capital Asset Pricing Model (CAPM): Markowitz's work helped form the Capital Asset Pricing Model. CAPM assumes that investors demand compensation for bearing systematic risk by requiring a higher expected return compared to the risk-free rate. The difference between the expected market return and the risk-free rate is known as the market risk premium. Individual investors do not necessarily need to review the risk premium of securities if they invest in a diversified index, such as the S&P 500. CAPM assumes a rational market and linear relationships between risk and return, so certainly has limitations because markets may not be rational, especially over shorter intervals.

Summary

- You must determine your time preference for spending over saving if you want to preserve the buying power of your money in the future.
- Do not invest until you understand the risks and have the resolve to execute that plan when it is tested by the stock market.
- Objectively determine your risk tolerance with specificity. Your strategy must be customized to your preferences, not to subjective catch-all terms such as "conservative, moderate, growth, or income-oriented."
- Consult a qualified financial planner or your CPA to plan your finances beyond the investment of your assets.

NEW-ERA ADVISORY FIRM MODEL: PAY ONLY FOR WHAT YOU NEED

YOU CAN INVEST INDEPENDENTLY, engage an asset-based fee advisor and give them discretion to make portfolio changes, or hire a registered investment advisor as a coach or investment planner. If you want to invest independently but would like professional advice with planning and portfolio composition, as well as documented short- and long-term portfolio projections and a statement of investment policy, you may want to explore the fixed-fee, limited engagement of a consultative arrangement offered by my firm. After initial engagement, the firm is available for check-in consultations.

Why New Era? My new firm is simply an extension of the institutional consulting model designed to determine investment risk tolerance and long-term investment planning for individual investors for a one-time fixed fee, unlike other registered advisers that charge ongoing asset-based fees. I believe it to be unique and possibly disruptive to the entrenched practices of existing registered investment advisory firms, or wealth management firms, as they like to be known. After all, long-term stock investing benefits most from holding positions, not from active trading or trying to game the equity market, as fun and exciting as that may seem to some. The other significant fact is that most registered investment advisors and mutual funds have not persistently outperformed their relevant equity benchmark indices, despite charging fees for attempting to do so.

Index funds, usually in the form of ETFs, offer a cogent alternative, for a low cost. Reducing or eliminating management fees is a significant saving for clients, especially when compounded. It presents a simplified, independent, and objective approach to investment planning, portfolio analysis, and implementation to reduce the frictional costs of legacy, asset-based fee advisory firms. Of course, the existing asset-based fee advisory firms could unbundle their services to provide only those necessary to establish a durable strategy, deliver a documented record of the specific client risk and return preferences, propose a portfolio, draft an investment policy statement, and then be available for brief, fixed fee check-ins as requested. This would clearly disrupt the recurring, asset-based fee model. The multi-trillion-dollar wealth management industry will resist any change from their recurring fee, low capital-intensive operations. Indeed, they promote them aggressively because they represent a very high-profit margin business. A one percent annual fee is typical, in addition to the fees charged by mutual funds or ETFs that the advisor may purchase, resulting in fees well above one percent a year. Although anecdotal, some brokerage firms want their representatives to generate 3% a year or more from the assets under their discretion. If the brokerage and investment advisory industry provided transparency about all the fees that they charge a client, we would all be in a better position to make a choice.

Given the many inquiries I have received since retirement, I decided to offer a new model advisory firm where investors pay only for what they need, not ongoing supervision of a portfolio that is unlikely to require frequent changes. Those who inquired about me told me that they trust their advisors because the account value has increased. They rarely ask, or certainly have not told me how much of the increase was simply due to the stock market advance and how much was due to manager skill and value-added above the broad stock market after advisor fees. More than a few people have told me that their advisor has made them "a lot" of money and I am too polite to ask, "Compared to what?" Their common sentiment is that the financial market is too complicated, so they ignore it and lean on their advisor to apprise them of their progress. Indeed, the media narrative, especially the financial media, presents us with information that can be bewildering, chaotic, and even frightening for the average individual investor. Perhaps these investors have enough assets to never be concerned with a decline in their value, or they may have a very specific measure of their tolerance for a decline in the value of their portfolio. That would be quite unusual in my professional experience.

Our risk and return preference assessment relies on a highly analytical framework, pairing mathematical sophistication with a more visually responsive client experience and accessible language to clarify the relationship between investment risk and reward.

The risk tolerance questionnaire tests prior assumptions and challenges them for accuracy. Each question is based on the math of the prior questions. The calculations are made in the cloud on an encrypted platform.

Each questionnaire starts with a relevant dollar amount and proceeds to an interactive module that begins the measurement of the investor's comfort zone. This sliding scale around the dollar amount to be invested has 158 gradations. The series of dynamic gamble/guarantee scenarios that follow include 966 trillion paths through the risk assessment.

The assessment begins with a few fact-finding questions that allow investors the chance to share their goals, financial status, and when they plan to retire. Broad categories are retirement, college savings, wealth accumulation, paying down debt, income, or a custom goal. The next step is an open-ended question about financial status, including employment, inheritances, or major expenses, for example. Next is the investor's dollar amount. There is nothing more critical to the accuracy and effectiveness of the risk questionnaire than this value because it allows the investor to focus on the consequences of their preferences. It will shape the rest of the questionnaire, which is dynamic and based on the previous responses. The actual value determines each subsequent question and presents return and risk trade-offs. The next question is the investor's age which is used in the longer-term planning projections. Next are questions to gauge the investor's financial sentiment, such as how they feel about the market and their financial future and provide insight into the investor's emotional connection to the assets.

Our process also calculates six-month and longer-term return probabilities considering inputs such as expected contributions, payments, and inflation, for example. We refer to this report as a retirement map that calculates the probable range of values over the relevant time horizon for that client. The client defines withdrawal and contribution values as well as when they may want to begin making withdrawals, as well as their inflation assumption. The determination of a comfort zone is the best way to quantify the suitability of a program for the investor.

We prepare an investment policy statement that expresses the objectives and presents a framework for a review of the strategy. The investor can implement changes as necessary, perhaps after a brief check-in consultation, and, in the process, save thousands of dollars in fees. Investors can also derive satisfaction when the outcome of their strategy delivers the desired results, especially if they adhere to their strategy in the inevitable interval when it will be tested by a stock market decline. The aggregate savings nationally of such an approach would probably be hundreds of millions of dollars annually, but more importantly, the compounded benefit would accrue to the investor. Of course, many are influenced by the aspirational and ubiquitous advertising of the major mutual fund and brokerage firms and are led to believe that they are incapable of producing the returns that allow the people in the advertisements to live in ideal circumstances. You may notice that the attractive advertising is designed to create an image and visualization of financial freedom and a carefree life, but it does not address the process the firm advocates for its clients or how exactly it adds measurable value. We are supposed to infer that the firm can produce wonderful results and, in the process, allow us to be carefree because of their assumed acumen, size, and the acceptance of millions of customers. It would be interesting if those firms would disclose the typical cumulative fees that such apparently successful, though apocryphal clients, would have paid over a specific time period and how they relate to the final value that delivers the aspirational lives that they apparently live. Some advertisements suggest that the firm is unique because it only makes more money when the client does and does not sell "products" or charge commissions, which may be true but are nonetheless specious, as we discuss below. A "product" is a tangible object with a shelf life. Investing is a service or process, even if it is within a mutual fund, ETF, or other vehicles offered by a sponsor. The terms in the investment industry may seem odd to the non-investment professional because they are. They add to the confusion that everyday people may have about the industry.

In summary, my new firm focuses on the individual's preferences for return and risk on an objective basis using an iterative series of questions that are related to dollar value currently and prospectively. We do not use subjective terms to define a client, such as capital preservation, conservative, moderate, aggressive, or income oriented. It also involves personal face-to-face interaction and affords the client the opportunity to ask any questions they wish and to get my perspective and advice.

Our questionnaire to determine risk and return preferences produces a risk score that is expressed in numbers between 0 and 99, and a range of probable returns in dollar terms around the client's current portfolio value over a six-month horizon. For reference, the S&P 500 currently has a risk score of 75. Of course, we also project longer-term ranges of returns. The reason for the six-month view is to set expectations realistically within 95% probability designed to keep clients on track with their strategy and minimize uncertainty. We determine the client's portfolio risk score and calibrate it with their desired risk score and if necessary, propose changes that would have the desired risk score. Clients may request check-in meetings should they have questions after their portfolio implementation. The investment advisory industry practices and fees have not changed with technological advances and are vulnerable to disruption, which is what I advocate is in the best interest of clients.

Summary

- A fixed fee investment planning model with access to check-ins serves the individual investor more efficiently than an asset-based fee arrangement.
- Asset-based fee advisors will be disrupted by a more efficient model that will save individual investors millions or even billions of dollars annually.
- The multi-trillion-dollar wealth management industry will resist any change from their recurring fee and low capital-intensive operations, and they promote them aggressively.

IS WALL STREET YOUR FRIEND?

If you ask the right questions Wall Street can be your friend, or if you do not ask, you do not get.

WALL STREET and the investment industry provide a means for us to allocate capital, grow the economy, save, invest for retirement, and offer the opportunity to maintain or improve our standard of living after inflation. It may do so in an especially promotional way, which underscores the importance of maintaining perspective and information on topics that matter most to you as an individual investor, a steward of funds for others in your family, or if you are on a governing board.

What changes have occurred in the industry as technology has driven down costs, and how has it changed the way the investment firms are paid and the fees that their customers pay? How have the changes benefited individual investors? We have all benefited from disruption in major industries over the past twenty years or so that we use daily, from rapid delivery of goods, mobile devices, and other advances that have changed the way we live and have saved us time and money. Despite the many changes in our economy and business models, Wall Street stubbornly clings to the high-profit margin business with recurring fees, with no capital requirement that asset management offers. It does to date not feel compelled to define or advertise how it adds value after its fees to the investing public.

The typical fee model in the investment management industry is to charge based on a percentage of assets under management. This means that a hypothetical client with $500,000 under management may pay 1% a year for advisory services. This fee is in addition to any mutual fund or exchange-traded fund fees that the client may own. Some advisors buy individual securities, so there is no additional charge to the client over the management fee, but then the question is how tax efficient is the individual portfolio, and how has it performed after fees relative to typical market benchmarks like the S&P 500? If the assets grow at the historical rate of growth in recent years of about 7%, the assets will double in about ten years and the fee would go from $5,000 a year to $10,000 a year, or 1% on a million-dollar portfolio. Several states require that the advisor send at least quarterly advice on fees charged to client custody accounts, but not all, so clients may be unaware of the thousands of dollars that they pay the advisor. Long-term investors benefit from low portfolio turnover so save on taxes, and in any event a well-designed and diversified portfolio need not change much or at all over time. Advisors with discretion can rebalance the portfolio after significant market changes back to strategy allocation levels, but that is usually only occasional and typically not more than once in three to five years. Recall that Warren Buffett has said that his favorite holding period for an investment is "forever." The question then is: What additional services or value does the investment advisor add in those ten years that deserve a doubling in compensation? Some advisors provide year-end tax harvesting strategies, but those are typically not significant, and if they are the advisor should quantify their added value. For many clients the comfort factor, not necessarily uncommon investment acumen, and performance of an otherwise friendly advisor is worth the additional fee, but not for all.

Institutional investors have for many years engaged consultants and pay fixed fees only for what they need for advice on investment planning and implementation, not ongoing supervision of their portfolios. While clients can request services such as performance reports or trading costs, custodians for individuals provide a variety of portfolio monitoring services for no additional cost to the client, which is a major change from the past. The fixed-fee approach, not unlike the way that other professionals like medical doctors, dentists, attorneys, and CPAs charge clients, seems more appropriate to me, and, in any event, would result in materially lower fees that the client pays over the term of the investment program. Why should the advisor benefit from financial market growth over time? To make matters worse, many advisors acquire a "book of business" over time, and then sell it along with its annual fees to a buyer for a significant amount of money, and usually multiples of annual revenue. Clients must agree to ownership changes so their account is not automatically transferred to the successor firm and owner. Do clients participate in such windfalls? Advisors value such "sticky" client assets from their clients for a simple reason.

Summary

- How does Wall Street add value to your assets?
- How have individual investors benefited from lower costs due to technological advances and competition?
- You should not pay more management fees as your assets grow.

- How does the client benefit when a wealth manager sells their book of business for a multiple of asset management fee revenues?

INVESTMENT PROFESSIONALS

Financial Advisor, Investment Advisor, Financial Planner, and Broker—What do they do? What certifications do they have?

Financial Advisor

The term "financial advisor" can refer to those with different professional credentials and regulatory approval. Broadly, a financial advisor provides guidance and advice regarding various financial decisions that can encompass investment strategies, retirement planning, budgeting, tax planning, insurance, and estate planning. Financial advisors can work independently or as part of financial institutions, brokerage firms, banks, insurance companies, or other financial service companies. The title "financial advisor" does not necessarily include registered investor advisor representatives. They may hold various certifications or licenses, such as Certified Financial Planner (CFP), Chartered Financial Analyst (CFA), or Registered Investment Advisor (RIA).

Registered Investment Advisor

Registered investment advisors (RIA) offer investment planning, management services, and account reporting and typically offer or have arrangements for custody of client assets with qualified custodians and are fiduciaries. Advisors should disclose that the law requires them to be fiduciaries, and that they are not special because they are fiduciaries. All registered investment advisory (RIA) firm entities are under regulatory supervision either by the Securities and Exchange Commission of the United States (SEC) or each state securities regulator, depending upon the size and nature of each firm's business. The regulatory framework is rigorous but does not guarantee safety for investors. All advisors are fiduciaries and must put the client's best interest before their own or their firms. RIA firms typically charge annual fees based on the assets under management of a client but may also be paid commissions on securities trades and/or marketing fees paid by mutual funds, known as 12 (b) 1 fees. Typically, annual investment management fees are 1% of a client's assets under advisement or management by the RIA, although some may charge a higher or lower percentage of assets or may have graduated fees with a lower percentage charge for assets above certain amounts. The fee is in addition to fees that the investor will pay to mutual funds, ETFs, and transaction commissions that the advisor may incur for the client. All fees must be disclosed, and clients should receive statements of all account activity, including all fees that they paid the advisor at least quarterly based on regulatory requirements.

There are two broad categories of advisors. The first is independent advisors who may select investment vehicles with no obligation—or incentive to favor one mutual fund sponsor or brokerage firm over another. The second type of advisor is captive and operates under an arrangement with a brokerage firm or mutual fund whose financial vehicles to which they may be restricted, whether they are the most competitive in all respects or not. It is important to understand whether and how your advisor can select the most suitable investments if their choices are limited. There may be hybrid advisors, but the basic distinction between independent and captive is operative.

There is no requirement for advisors to report the value that they objectively and quantifiably add to client accounts. If they did such reporting clients would have the information necessary for decisions about retaining or releasing their advisor. There are ratings for mutual funds that are available from third-party firms, such as Morningstar, which conduct a rigorous analysis of each fund. Of course, ratings may change, or the mutual fund strategy may encounter a less hospitable environment, so it is important when reviewing ratings to understand the appropriate context of the strategy and its investment time horizon. A fund manager may also change, which may negate or modify a prior rating and analysis. A particular fund strategy or style may be in favor for years, but there is no guarantee that the environment will remain salutary because investment fashion changes and will continue to change. This has been true in the recent decade which has favored high-revenue growth company shares to the detriment of slower-growing, so-called value company shares. For example, for the ten years that ended June 30, 2023, the S&P 500 Growth Index generated a total rate of annualized return of 14.49% while the S&P 500 Value Index produced 10.51% a year. The total S&P 500 generated 12.86% a year for the same ten years. Advisors managing individual stocks generally favor investment styles ranging from growth to value, large and medium-capitalization, and small-capitalization, as well as some who favor specific industries of economic sectors. Most investors favor those managers who adhere closely to their chosen style and do not display "style drift."

You may find testimonials about advisors from their clients, which have only recently been permitted by the SEC and state regulators, provided certain disclosures are included. We all want validation of our preferences, so testimonials and direct references may be helpful as one considers engaging an advisor. The Internet has made third-party ratings available for all manner of goods and services, typically highlighting star ratings. Unless such ratings can be validated as authentic, be aware that they may not be real. Advisors have a legal and fiduciary responsibility to keep all client information confidential, so an advisor would have to obtain authorization from each client to make a reference available. If an advisor is unwilling to provide specific client references, a potential client may want to look for those who will.

Advisors' asset-based annual fees increase with market value appreciation, and some have graduated fee schedules that may scale down for larger accounts. In my years of performing due diligence on RIAs, I never came across one that charged flat fees not dependent on asset value for account management, although they may exist. Typical advisory agreement terms are open-ended and subject to client cancellation on thirty days' notice with a rebate of any fees usually paid in advance. Industry practice tends to accept client notice of release immediately, stop trading, and refund unearned fees with no waiting period. Fees must be negotiable, according to regulations. It should be clear that clients of RIAs pay fees daily whether there is activity by the advisor or not. Most advisors declare that they have continuous supervision of client assets, which implies that they evaluate a client's portfolio daily or make frequent portfolio changes. Prospective clients should inquire about the frequency of portfolio changes and whether they have added value, especially if the changes are made in a taxable account where sale proceeds will be less after taxes are paid on gains. Strategies that realize short-term gains are subject to higher tax rates than those that realize long-term gains. It is important to understand the cost of taxes because taxes reduce the amount available for reinvestment.

RIAs are subject to strict performance presentation reporting requirements. Investors should examine the past performance of an RIA relative to the relevant index benchmark of its strategy to gauge if the advisor has added value and if so, how persistently the value has been added. If advisors do not present a compliant investment performance record for accounts like your prospective account, you probably should look for those who do. The excuse that an advisor's clients all have different objectives, therefore there is no comparable performance record available sounds evasive to me. Moreover, clients with similar objectives should be managed consistently with little or no variation in performance among different client accounts. Investors should heed the disclaimers that past performance is not necessarily an indication of future results, although the tendency to extrapolate past performance into the future is often the case. It is usually the case that investors expect the superior performance to continue, despite the regulator's familiar and required disclaimer.

In addition to investment advisors who provide discretionary management services of client assets with discretion, there are investment advisors who offer their services on a non-discretionary basis. Institutional and family investment offices have engaged non-discretionary advisors, typically known as investment consultants, for many years. More recently, institutional investors have engaged chief investment officers, known as outsourced CIOs, or OCIOs, who typically have investment discretion. The OICO can implement its investment decisions efficiently without the need to get approval from the fund sponsor. All fiduciaries remain responsible for the prudent investment and stewarding of funds under their purview, so delegating that responsibility does not relieve the fiduciary of responsibility.

What I propose to individuals is that they follow what institutions have done and engage an investment consultant to assist them with investment planning, strategy, and implementation, but not discretionary management of the portfolio. Rather than paying for the ongoing management services of an investment advisor or ICIO, a more efficient approach is to pay the consultant a one-time fixed fee for planning, strategy, drafting an investment policy statement, and objectively determining the client's investment time horizon, return goals, and risk tolerance in specific dollar terms using probability analysis. The fact is that institutions have used probability analysis successfully for years. The most recent version of probability analysis that my firm uses is based on the Nobel Prize-winning work of Daniel Kahneman's Prospect Theory. Technology has made such analysis accessible and more affordable than in the recent past. There is no need to pay more than once for the same advice, particularly when the client portfolio requires no changes to their allocations because they are long-term investors. The most important part of investing is to establish a strategy and framework for diligent review and then construct a portfolio that aligns with the objective using probability analysis.

RIAs are regulated by the SEC or state administrators or both. There are no required certifications for investment advisors except that they pass the requisite tests administered by an industry self-regulatory body, the Financial Industry Regulatory Authority (FINRA). The history of each advisor is publicly available on the FINRA site, through the SEC broker check web search function, or the SEC's Investment Advisor Public Disclosure website, www.

adviserinfo.sec.gov. Each advisory firm should have readily available links to its regulatory filings to make it easier for the public to review its history and other relevant factors.

Many advisors are Chartered Financial Analysts (CFAs). The CFA designation is a rigorous series of three exams and is generally regarded as the highest form of certification an individual may have as an investment professional. I have never seen the effectiveness ratings of CFAs compared to non-CFAs as investment decision-makers, but the assumption is that a CFA adheres to high ethical standards and is exempt from the requirement to pass the FINRA exams. The fact is that compliance is essential at all levels of an investment advisory entity, and all advisors and certain staff are required to adhere to the regulations, subject to severe penalties for non-compliance.

Financial Planners

Financial planners offer a full range of services and may also be registered as investment advisors. A financial planner may have a professional designation, typically as a Certified Financial Planner (CFP). They would start a plan by reviewing a person's financial profile including assets, liabilities, income, savings and investments, retirement goals, tax bracket, insurance, and other risk management considerations, business planning, retirement plan structures, and legacy planning. Financial planners typically charge a flat fee for planning and perhaps implementation. Financial planners often are licensed insurance producers for life and health types of policies, so they may be paid insurance policy commissions. It should be noted that Certified Public Accountants (CPAs) often provide holistic financial planning for their clients and are usually the client's most trusted advisor, after perhaps their physician.

Brokers and Broker-Dealers

Brokers and broker-dealers facilitate securities transactions and are licensed by FINRA and must pass rigorous tests. They must adhere to specific regulations imposed by the SEC. Brokers do not owe a fiduciary duty to their clients. Therefore, they may not necessarily work in the client's best interests, although they have been subject to the SEC Regulation BI since June 30, 2020. There are no other academic or professional certifications necessary to be a broker, financial planner, or investment advisor. Brokers can execute authorized trade orders for clients who have accounts that meet the brokerage firm's requirements. They are typically paid based on commissions that they generate, or sometimes receive salaries, from their firms and incentive compensation.

Brokers are individuals who facilitate the execution of trades for their clients. Brokers do not hold or take ownership of the securities being traded; instead, they connect buyers and sellers and charge a commission or fee for their services.

Broker-dealers are firms or institutions that perform both brokerage and dealer functions. In addition to facilitating trades for clients as brokers, they also engage in proprietary trading as dealers. As dealers, they buy and sell securities for their own accounts, and they may hold inventory for short-term trading purposes.

Regulation BI (Best Interest)

Regulation Best Interest (Regulation BI or Reg BI) is a set of rules established by the SEC that became effective on June 30, 2020, and is designed to enhance investor protection and provide greater transparency and clarity in the relationship between investors and broker-dealers. Brokers must disclose a narrative that describes their policies regarding the regulation. The standard requires broker-dealers to act in the best interest of their customers and to avoid conflicts of interest that could compromise the impartiality of their recommendations.

Broker-dealers are required to consider the customer's investment profile, including their financial situation, investment objectives, risk tolerance, and other relevant factors when making a recommendation, and to disclose any potential conflicts of interest that could influence their recommendations. Further, they must exercise reasonable diligence, care, skill, and prudence to understand the potential risks and rewards of a recommendation, and to have a reasonable basis for believing it is in the best interest of the customer. Finally, they must establish, maintain, and enforce written policies and procedures designed to identify, disclose, and mitigate or eliminate conflicts of interest associated with their recommendations.

Investors should be mindful that brokers and broker-dealers are not fiduciaries, unlike RIAs, who have a fiduciary duty to act in the best interest of their clients. While Regulation BI is an improvement, investors need to remain aware of potential conflicts of interest and thoroughly understand the fees, risks, and benefits associated with any investment recommendations they receive from broker-dealers.

INVESTMENT CHOICES
Stocks, Bonds, Index Funds, Mutual Funds, Hedge Funds, Commodities, and Savings Accounts

Corporate Capital Structure

Corporations finance operations and growth through a combination of debt (bonds) and equity (stock). Typically, corporations have a combination of long-term debt, short-term loans, preferred stock, and common equity. The balance between debt and equity depends on numerous factors, including cash flow generation, growth prospects, and the cost of capital, and ideally maximizes shareholder value while financing corporate growth with flexibility and efficiency.

Debt may include short and long-term borrowings. Interest payments on debt are tax deductible.

Equity represents ownership in the company. Common equity consists of common shares issued to shareholders. Preferred equity is a hybrid security that sits between debt and common equity, offering fixed dividends like debt but no maturity date.

Stocks

Stocks, also called equities, represent a portion of the ownership of a corporation. As such they represent the earning power of the corporation and net worth of a corporation, and its ability to produce a return for its shareholders in the form of dividends and/ or increasing the value of the enterprise. The price of a stock is reflected by its trading on regulated exchanges and is influenced by a variety of factors. The determinants of value vary considerably but depend on the quality of a company's financial stability, growth, and prospects for a company's earning power. Equities can go to zero value and are junior to all other corporate securities, such as bonds in the event of a company liquidation. The reason to own equity is that corporate management is incented to produce adequate returns for shareholders. On balance, corporations have generated returns to shareholders that compensate for the risk of owning them. If corporations do not generate increasing value for the enterprise or pay out dividends there is no reason to own them. Investors look to the future earnings or other fundamental value properties of a company. Prices of stocks can vary considerably based on specific company prospects, current or expected interest rates, and investor sentiment about earnings growth or the economy, among many other factors. Over the long term, stocks have provided the best liquid price inflation hedge despite their sometimes dramatic declines in price. Common stockholders can vote on certain corporate matters as designated by their respective boards of directors in accordance with the law.

Equities that pay dividends will typically do so quarterly. Not all corporations pay dividends and there is no guarantee that those that do pay common stock dividends will sustain them, much less grow them. An ideal stock is one of a company that increases its dividend and sustains sufficient capital to invest in its future.

Preferred stocks pay dividends semi-annually but may have restricted voting rights. By investing in convertible preferred stocks, investors can gain exposure to both the equity and fixed-income markets within a single security, offering potential diversification benefits. There are straight preferred and convertible preferred stocks that may have attractive features depending on the investor's preferences. Preferred stocks typically pay fixed dividends, providing a more predictable income stream for investors. These dividends are paid before common stock dividends, which can be attractive to income-seeking investors. In the event of a company's liquidation or bankruptcy, preferred stockholders have higher priority than common stockholders in receiving their share of the company's assets. Preferred stocks tend to exhibit lower price volatility compared to common stocks. Their prices are influenced more by changes in interest rates and credit quality than by prospects for the company's earnings or market sentiment. Some preferred stocks offer tax advantages. Dividends from qualified preferred stocks may be taxed at a lower rate than ordinary income, providing tax efficiency for certain investors.

Convertible preferred stocks include an option that allows the holder to convert their preferred shares into a predetermined number of common shares at a specified conversion price. This feature can be attractive if the company's common stock performs well, allowing investors to benefit from potential capital appreciation. They offer a balance of fixed income (from the preferred dividend) and potential capital appreciation (if the conversion option is exercised). Whether the conversion option is exercised or not, convertible stocks offer fixed dividends and higher priority in corporate liquidation. Since the conversion option provides some equity-like characteristics, they may be less affected by fluctuations in interest rates.

Warrants are standalone securities that give the holder the right to buy a specified number of common shares of a company at a predetermined price (the exercise or strike price) within a specified timeframe. Companies often issue them to raise capital when issuing other securities like bonds or preferred stock. They can be detachable, which means they can be traded separately from the underlying security, or they can be attached to other securities, like preferred stock or bonds.

Bonds

Bonds are a debt obligation of a corporation and are typically used to finance longer-term business investments. There are a variety of bond types, including convertible bonds that may be converted to common shares of the issuing company. Bonds are also issued by state and local entities as well as revenue authorities and are termed "municipal bonds." Municipal bonds are generally exempt from federal income taxes but are subject to state income tax for non-resident owners. Bondholders have rights in a corporate liquidation that can vary based on other creditor claims. Bonds pay coupon interest semi-annually and when purchased, the buyer must pay accrued interest from the most recent coupon interest payment. Bonds are issued in one-thousand-dollar denominations referred to as par value and their market price is expressed as a percentage of par value, such that a bond trading at $900 is quoted as 90. U.S. Treasury Bills, Notes, and bonds are issued regularly by the U.S. Treasury for maturities of 13, 26, and 52 weeks as well as two, five, ten, and thirty-year maturities respectively. U.S. Treasuries are the highest quality credit that one can purchase.

Corporations may also issue commercial paper that is typically offered in large denominations, is unsecured debt, and has a maximum maturity of 270 days. Ratings agencies issue grades or ratings to such unsecured debt, and it falls within the money market category of assets. Other money market assets are short-term U.S. Treasury and Agency securities with maturities of less than a year and may also include bank repurchase agreements or other types of short-term commercial financing vehicles. Efficient, although not cost-free, access to such money market instruments is typically through money market mutual funds that offer daily liquidity and a promise to maintain their dollar value. Some money market funds did not maintain their dollar value in the wake of the Great Financial Crisis in 2008-2009. This unfortunate event is termed "breaking the buck" and in some cases caused issuers to suspend redemptions in the wake of the Great Financial Crisis.

It is essential for investors in bonds to understand their yields to maturity and their duration, which is a measure of a bond's sensitivity to changes in yield to maturity as well as embedded options like call terms and prepayment. The price of bonds with higher duration will fluctuate more than those with lower duration. The price of bonds moves inversely with interest rates, such that increases in interest rates will mean a lower price. For example, if the duration of a bond is ten years and interest rates were to change by 1% the price of the bond would change by approximately 10%. If this hypothetical bond traded at a par value of $1,000, it would appreciate about 10% to $110 if the interest rate declined by 1% and would decline in market value to $90 if interest rates increased by 1%. There are a variety of other risks in owning bonds that must be reviewed, including quality, options such as calls and puts, and a bond's relationship to similar bonds available in the market.

It is also important to consider reinvestment risk. Lower interest rates at that bond's maturity will reduce the attractiveness of opportunities to reinvest the proceeds. A common mistake can be buying bonds with the highest yield to maturity or "chasing yield" without considering the possibility of a rise in yields to maturity that will cause the bond's value to decline. If held to maturity the holder will receive their par value, unless of course there is a default.

Perhaps is it worth noting that when entities like banks borrow money and pay interest on the borrowing, the proceeds might be invested in securities or loans with longer maturities than the maturity of the borrowed funds or deposits in banks. Banks must maintain reserves against deposits, but as we have seen, the reserves may be insufficient to offset a decline in the asset values of the bank's securities or loans. It the investments yield more than the borrowed funds cost the difference is called a positive "spread." This is good if the value of the investments or loans maintain their value. If interest rates rise a mismatch in maturities will lead to diminished value and would have to be sold at a loss to meet deposit withdrawals and the difference would have to be made up with liquid capital. This asset/liability mismatch was the cause of bank failures in the spring of 2023 when those banks invested funds in maturities that were longer, sometimes much longer, than the maturity of the borrowed funds, or in the bank's cases, depositors' money. Those banks' reserves were insufficient to make up the difference. Depositors, even those with a billion dollars on deposit, were made whole by the government in the recent bank failures. The reason for this is probably that the government accommodated depositors because it wanted to stem a "run" on other banks by depositors.

Index Funds and Exchange Traded Funds (ETFs)

Index funds, often referred to as "passive" vehicles, invest in designated indices, which may include equities or bonds or other securities such as real estate. Indices are constructed to track a group of securities. The most common index is the S&P 500. The

Dow Jones Industrial Average is another benchmark that is less diversified than the S&P 500 and probably the best-known benchmark. The most popular way to invest in index funds is through Exchange Traded Funds although they are also offered in mutual funds. ETFs trade on securities exchanges throughout each trading session, while mutual funds trade only once each trading session and are priced after each day's close of markets. The popularity of ETFs has increased significantly, as investors favor their low fee structure. They also have tax advantages that mutual funds do not. Hundreds of indices represent a broad variety of industries and geographic sectors. The fees charged by index fund sponsors, typically mutual fund companies, are generally low compared to managed mutual funds. Some ETFs are managed because the sponsor has engaged an advisor to execute a specific strategy, often in a sector of the economy, such as energy or healthcare, that an investor may want to use for diversification. ETFs also offer strategies that profit if the underlying securities decline in value, but investors need to read each prospectus as they define the structure of the strategy. Managed ETFs usually have higher expense ratios (fees).

Some ETFs charge extremely low or no fees for broad exposure to the equity markets and are generally recognized as prudent approaches if, for no other reason, the fees are low while providing efficient diversification. The low fees can be quite significant over the long term. Also, most mutual funds that are managed do not consistently outperform the broad stock market indices.

Mutual Funds

A mutual fund is organized under the Investment Company Act of 1940 and aggregates assets for investment in specific funds and strategies. Mutual funds were started to offer investors access to vehicles that were typically diversified and managed by professionals. Each investor in a mutual fund owns a proportionate share of the total fund. They are governed by independent boards of directors. The prices of mutual funds are determined at the market close daily. Mutual funds charge annual fees based on the assets under management. Each fund publishes the expense ratio as a percentage of fund assets for the fees that it charges, which includes all management, administrative, and marketing fees incurred by the fund. Expense ratios may vary widely depending on the fund's strategy and management arrangement.

Short Selling

If an investor believes that the price of a stock will decline, they may borrow shares from a broker, if they have a margin account, and then sell those borrowed shares hoping to buy them back or "cover" their short at a lower price and repay the loan of those shares. The proceeds of the short sale are deposited with the broker and earn an interest rate. The short seller must pay the dividends received to the owner of the borrowed shares. The risks of short-selling strategies may be considerable and not symmetrical with prospective gains. A stock can go to zero or to a much higher price, at which the short seller may have to buy them back to cover or repay their borrowed shares. A long position in a $10 stock exposes the owner to a potential loss of $10, if that stock goes to $20, they double their money, or if it goes to $30, they triple their money. If one borrows a $10 a share stock and sells, the most that they can make is 100% if the stock goes to zero, but if the stock appreciates to $20, they will lose 100% of their money and may have to post additional collateral as the stock appreciates. What if the stock trades at $30 or more? They must purchase shares at $30 to repay their borrowed stock. You get the picture. It is said that there are no bears who live on Park Avenue, so while we hear about the successful short sellers on the financial news networks, they are very rare. There is nothing sweeter for an investor to make money in a down market, but it is exceedingly difficult to do and should be prudently viewed typically as a modest hedge in a long stock program. Also, there is no shortage of those who express negative outlooks for the stock market, rarely citing their track record of predictions, but fear sells so they get publicity, usually without any disclosure of their effectiveness. Such short sellers often "talk their book" to promote others to sell stocks and drive the price down. It is against regulations to disclose specific positions publicly.

Hedge Funds

Hedge funds are registered as private placements under Regulation D of the Securities Act of 1933 and are generally not available to the public, although some mutual funds execute hedged strategies of various types and are available to the public. The private placements are only available to accredited investors or qualified purchasers. Funds available to accredited investors, also known as 3(c)1 funds may have ninety-nine limited partners, while those available to qualified purchasers, also known as 3(c)7 funds, may have 499 limited partners. Individuals can qualify as accredited investors if their annual income exceeds $200,000 for single individuals or $300,000 for married couples filing jointly for the recent two calendar years, and the income is expected to remain at or above that level in the current year. The individual's net worth is at least $1 million, excluding their primary residence and certain financial professionals. A qualified purchaser is defined under the Investment Company Act of 1940. To qualify as a qualified purchaser an individual must have at least $5 million in investments, and certain family-owned companies with at least $5 million in investments, or certain trusts that are not formed for the specific purpose of acquiring the securities being offered and have total assets of at least $5 million.

Hedge funds became popular in the 1990s and generally were sought by those who wanted a higher return than possible in conventional long investing in stocks. The classical hedge fund before they became popular was long and short stocks and depended on stock selection to extract a premium over the market return. The typical fee structure included an annual fee based on a percentage of the assets in the fund and an incentive allocation. Generally, the fees have been between 1% and 2% of assets for management, plus 20% of the profits after the management fee, usually after attaining a recovery to the latest high value or "high-water mark," should the fund decline. The fee and incentive structure of hedge funds attracted many sponsors and investors with the promise of a predictable return stream. That the basic structure has persisted, albeit with management fees often being reduced as well as the incentive allocation of 20%, is notable.

Hedge Funds Can be Fee Machines

The term "hedge fund" has been applied to many vehicles that have basically the same legal structure and fee terms. No two hedge funds that I have seen execute the same strategy, although there are many that are nominally similar. The fee structure for hedge funds as described above has two components: a management fee of 1% to 2% and sometimes higher, plus incentive compensation for gains produced of usually 20%. The fees are an accident of history and are common in the industry, although have been reduced somewhat in recent years. Most hedge funds do not charge incentive compensation fees until an account balance recovers any depreciation or exceeds the so-called high-water mark. The more desirable fee structure is of course lower management and incentive fees, but most importantly has a hurdle rate below which the hedge fund gets no incentive compensation. The hurdle rate may be an absolute number like 10% or the S&P 500 return for the year for which the incentive is calculated. Most hedge funds have no hurdle rate which means that they receive the incentive or performance-based compensation annually for any return after the management fee is charged. Let us assume that the gross return is 10% and the management fee is 1%, with a 20% performance or incentive fee. The gross is reduced by 1% to 9%, and the 20% is charged to the 9% return, or 1.8% of the increase in the investor balance from the prior period, which in most cases is one year. The manager gets 2.8% of the investor's account in fees, so the investor has a net return of 7.2%. Another way to look at this is that the manager gets 28% of the gross or before the management fee and incentive fee return, and the investor gets 72%. The fees move beyond tolerably reasonable when the gross return is less and there is no hurdle rate above which the manager is entitled to incentive compensation of 20% in this example. If the gross return is only 6% the manager gets 1% in management fees and 20% of 5.0%, or 1.0% in incentive compensation, for a total of 2.0%, leaving the investor with a net return of 4.0%. In this example, the manager receives 33% of the gross return of 6% in fees and incentive payments. When hedge funds perform well above 10% gross return a year the fees may not appear to be too high, but when below they are difficult to justify.

Many hedge funds did not perform well in the market decline from March 2000 to October 2002, otherwise known as the Dot Com Crash. This caused fund sponsors and investors to gravitate towards lower-risk hedged strategies, which did not capture the gains registered by the S&P 500 from October 2002 to October 2007, when the Great Financial Crises began to manifest in stock price declines. There were and are hedged funds that performed consistently well and delivered better than S&P 500 rates of return from March 2000 to October 2007 and beyond, but if they continue to operate many have been closed to new investors for years.

There is still an active investor interest in hedged strategies, despite the unfavorable fee structure and below S&P 500 performance for many. Hedge fund selection is an especially challenging endeavor but can be very rewarding for those whose due diligence and acumen are superior. Unfortunately, all too often hedge funds disappoint and their terms often prohibit liquidation for a year or more if they are "gated" by the general partner. "Gating" is when the general partner suspends redemption privileges. It is important to remember that the general partner(s) of a hedge fund typically have very broad discretion, and they are not generally transparent, so trust is essential. It is important to note that as recounted elsewhere in the book is the Bernie Madoff fraud. Madoff did not manage a hedge fund but maintained individual accounts for his investors that proved to be completely fabricated. In general, if a potential investor cannot meet the general partner(s) of a hedge fund to take that person's measure, they should avoid investing in that fund. Or at least that was my rule.

There are so-called market-neutral strategies that maintain roughly similar allocations to short positions and long positions of stocks typically in the same industries, hoping to profit from anomalies in pricing due to competitive business prospects for portfolio constituents. Often such strategies use significant leverage to increase the impact of successful positions, but leverage is a very sharp two-edged sword. There is little room for error and leverage may mean that a decline in the value of collateral leads to margin calls and essentially forced liquidation of a position. One experienced investor described market-neutral strategies as running in front of a freight train picking up nickels. One obviously cannot stumble and fall. Market-neutral funds have generally not been a good place to invest relative to short to intermediate-term U.S. Treasury security allocations. If a manager can demonstrate a persistent ability to extract a premium from pricing anomalies using market-neutral positioning great, but in many years of hedge fund research, I have found that their records were at best spotty. The promise of making money no matter what the market direction is enticing, but not so easy in practice, especially compared to relatively safe short to intermediate term U.S. Treasury notes.

Beware of strategies that use index funds to hedge individual stock positions, because the correlation of the stock to an index may not be sufficiently high to provide the desired hedge. In other words, the stock and the index may not trade in the same direction to the same degree at the same time, therefore providing no or limited hedge. Index allocations in a hedge fund reflect a low conviction position. Hedge funds should have high conviction in their research and security selection. It is important for investors to understand risk management in hedged, long, and short portfolios because as described above the risk of shorting is asymmetrical.

Leveraged Investing and Options

I do not address options or other forms of leveraged investing and hedging, such as capital structure arbitrage, statistical arbitrage, and merger arbitrage that often require significant leverage, as I do not believe that they are necessary for long-term success in a more conventional stock and bond strategy. Moreover, although owning options has finite risk, determining the right price to pay for either call or put options can be very difficult. Some advisors advocate writing call options against existing long stock positions to generate income, but this presents the risk that if the stock does well during the option term, the stock can be called away from the investor and defeats the purpose of long-term investing. The investor may also have to pay a tax on the gains from such sales.

Alternative Investments

Alternative investments or "alts" became a popular category as hedge funds gained in popularity after the Great Financial Crisis. The point is that they are seen as deriving their returns from sufficiently diverse sources than publicly traded equities and bonds. Therefore, it is believed their correlation to the core portfolio of most funds that are comprised of unhedged equity can be efficiently diversified by investment in "alts." Correlation is a measure of the frequency and extent of how one security, in this case, behaves relative to another. A low correlation measure, or coefficient, is considered desirable when one is structuring a portfolio because it reduces volatility, which is a salutary factor and can produce a higher risk-adjusted rate of return. Modern Portfolio Theory rests largely upon combining securities with low correlation to produce higher risk-adjusted returns, and although non-intuitive, works well when portfolio constituents behave as expected. Bonds, for example, have had a historical correlation to stocks that is relatively low, thus they have been very efficient as a diversifying component for the equity allocation. Although that correlation may vary and not produce the benefit sought, as in 2022 when bonds declined almost as much as stocks, investment-grade bonds have been a solid diversifier to stocks.

Alternatives include hedge funds of all types, real estate, commodities, private credit, distressed credit, and private equity at all stages from angel investment funds to buyout funds. There is a mutual fund category for so-called alternatives, but most are available only in private placement funds for accredited investors and qualified purchasers as described above in the Hedge Fund paragraphs.

Individual investors who are not accredited investors or qualified purchasers may participate in private equity and credit by investing in publicly traded companies that in turn invest in private equity and credit. Investments in such company stocks are liquid and reflect the acumen of the corporations that invest so represent a proxy for private investments. There are relatively few publicly traded surrogates that invest primarily in private equity or debt/credit opportunities.

Private equity and credit funds have been extremely popular among institutional investors. Private equity benefited from historically low interest rates in the years after the Great Financial Crisis of 2008-2009, but since the Federal Reserve began raising interest rates in March 2022 the prospective returns from such funds have been impaired. Private credit funds have become popular due to the demand for non-bank loans. Both types of private funds are most often only available to accredited investors or qualified purchasers, usually in the form of limited partnerships. Both also have been difficult to value, and the practical fact is that their values are reported with a lag from valuations in publicly traded securities, although they are impacted by market valuations of publicly traded securities. Such valuation dynamics have seemingly benefited the performance of investors, at least temporarily, in such funds after public markets decline. One cannot know exactly what one earned until the final distributions are made from such funds, as they typically have terms that can be, and often are, extended. Typical initial terms are for ten years, although successful funds may make final distributions before the initial term of the partnership. The other factor that investors should bear in mind is that their terms provide for capital calls as determined by the respective general partners. Investors subscribe to a fixed commitment and must meet capital calls in a timely manner or may be subject to penalties or forfeiture of their capital accounts. This has presented a problem when public equity markets decline substantially, as occurred in 2008. Declines in publicly traded equities have increased the committed allocations to private equity funds, perhaps beyond an investor's intended parameters.

The other dynamic of private equity funds is that the general partners have very broad discretion and can extend fund termination dates to continue to manage their portfolio companies and collect management fees in the process. Unlike the initial period during which the funds' charge fees based on the committed capital, after several years they charge based on assets that are invested, although there are likely more capital calls to be made to fund future investments or follow-on investments in portfolio companies.

Real Estate Investment Trusts (REITs) are another vehicle available to individual investors to participate in companies that distribute a significant portion of their earnings in dividends. They may track private investments in real estate over time and generally are interest rate sensitive, which means that their publicly traded prices tend to decline as interest rates increase. Allocations to REITs can provide diversification to equity index funds as well as generally higher dividend yields.

Master Limited Partnerships (MLPs) may also be publicly traded and derive their income from rents, royalties, or other forms of recurring and predictable revenue. MLPs became very attractive as interest rates declined after 2009 and produced handsome returns until interest began to rise materially. They declined significantly as interest rose.

Commodities

Commodities are a large sector of financial markets and include currencies, interest rates, physical commodities like petroleum-based products, agricultural products, and metals. Typically, commodities trade on regulated futures exchanges and are used by producers of physical commodities to hedge against adverse price changes when the products or commodities are available for delivery to end users. They are also used by traders who have no intention of ever taking delivery of the physical products. There is an old quip about trading sardines and eating sardines. Commodity Trading Advisors (CTAs) may offer their trading strategies in private placements. The tendency of commodities to increase in value during stock market declines or general inflationary intervals has attracted investors who want to diversify their stock market exposure. Commodity exposure may be available in ETFs or mutual funds, such as the ETF representing gold bullion. It is important to note that as the price of physical commodities increases so does the supply, as the cost of production becomes less than the market price. The increase in supply due to more production or the sale by existing holders has inevitably led to price declines. There is no structural return to commodities, such as dividends or interest payments, and they trade based on the expectations of investors so long-term holding may not be productive.

Bank Savings Accounts

Let us review the savings accounts that I addressed in other chapters. While the comfort of Federal Deposit Insurance Corporation (FDIC) coverage of smaller deposits is significant, it, like all insurance, has a cost. Banks must generate positive interest rate spreads to remain viable, which has meant that the interest rates that they pay yield less than the asset in which the banks invest, principally loans and high-grade bonds after their expenses and reserve requirements imposed by the regulators. The bottom line on savings accounts is that they have not maintained purchasing power after paying taxes on interest. In March of 2023, we witnessed the failure of several large banks that had negative interest rate spreads because interest rates increased at a historically rapid pace and the prices of their assets declined so that their sale would result in large losses and an inability to meet savings withdrawals. This is called asset-liability mismatch, which is a fundamental principle that bankers must observe, but did not. Their depositors got lucky when the Federal Government bailed them out, including some very large depositors with much more than the $250,000 otherwise insured by the FDIC.

Bitcoin

Bitcoin is a consensus currency and exists in a cryptographic protocol on a global network of multiple users that has been robust since its formation in 2009. Every transaction in Bitcoin is on an indelible public ledger known as the blockchain. Transactions cannot be altered and are accessible such that regulatory authorities or law enforcement entities can determine how much was transacted by the owner's or recipient's address. The popular press and some in public office have repeatedly said that Bitcoin's sole use is for criminal activity because it is anonymous. The United Nations has estimated that between 2% and 5% of global GDP ($1.6 to $4 trillion) annually is associated with money laundering and illicit activity. Other reports suggest that the proportion of illicit transactions conducted in cryptocurrency are much less than 2% to 5%. Criminals prefer to use a printed currency that is untraceable. This should not surprise anyone. Another misconception is that Bitcoin is the same as other cryptographic tokens. Bitcoin is not controlled by a centralized sponsor, as are all other crypto tokens. It has a programmed, finite supply, unlike other tokens and is fundamentally different.

It is a permissionless asset with no centralized sponsorship or authority. It is the only asset that I know for which there is a finite supply except for land. The finite supply is set at 21 million. Currently, there are about 19.5 million Bitcoins outstanding. The algorithm that governs the issuance of new Bitcoin is written to limit daily issuance currently to 900 Bitcoins a day. Every four years the daily supply is halved. The next halving will be in April 2024. And will reduce the supply to 450 Bitcoins a day. Bitcoin is issued by miners who must solve complex mathematical problems to be rewarded with Bitcoin. The computational capacity and speed can be expensive to maintain, although, like other computational capacities and speeds, advances have reduced the cost and increased the efficiency of solving such problems.

Other assets discussed above except for land may have an unlimited supply, which is true about the U.S. dollar which is a fiat currency. Fiat currency is issued at the discretion of the Federal Reserve Bank in the United States and central banks of other countries issue their own currency. One may consider the finite supply as an intrinsic value element, but even if not, the fact that more cannot be created regardless of its price is a potentially powerful factor. If supply can increase with the price of an asset, it usually will. As the price of a commodity increases the incentive to produce more increases. That cannot happen with bitcoin.

One can purchase Bitcoin through registered cryptocurrency brokers and hold it in custody at those firms. The preferred method of holding Bitcoin is on a cold storage device not continuously connected to the Internet. Each holder can be assigned a seed phase of twenty-four words and the user selects a password to access their account using the cold storage device. The loss of the seed phase words means the loss of Bitcoin. This reportedly has happened to early adopters, essentially reducing supply, although we do not know how much has been frozen by those who have lost their seed phrases or passwords. Such cold storage devices are much more secure than mobile devices that are connected to the Internet. Nothing is infallible and there are no guarantees. Like any other asset, legal authorities can seize Bitcoin regardless of how one stores it.

One vehicle for the public to purchase and hold bitcoin has been the Grayscale Bitcoin Trust which is registered and publicly traded. It has an annual fee of 2% and has traded at a substantial premium and discount since its formation. There have been several applications for spot bitcoin EFTs by established mutual fund sponsors that would trade in line with the market price of Bitcoin and will charge a fee for administration of the ETF. Bitcoin trades continuously and registered securities, like ETFs, trade only when markets are open during the business week. The applications are pending as this is written in late 2023 and the Securities and Exchange Commission may continue to deny issuance. There have been several applications for spot bitcoin ETFs for a decade, but all have been denied. The SEC approved ETFs based on Bitcoin futures contracts in 2021. One memorable denial of an application for a spot ETF was in March 2017 when Bitcoin was trading at approximately $1,000. The applicants were the Winklevoss brothers who were very early adopters of Bitcoin when it was trading for a few dollars a coin. Bitcoin has traded at well above $1,000 since 2017. Its price has been volatile, and it may be considered a speculation by investors. Large daily price changes should be expected if the price history of Bitcoin is a guide. The volatility, lack of regulatory clarity, and an inaccurate description of Bitcoin facts have dominated the narrative of popular financial and general media. Despite this conventional view of Bitcoin, two of the largest mutual fund sponsors have deemed Bitcoin to be a separate asset class. Although not persistently less correlated with stocks or bonds the finite nature of Bitcoin may support this argument. Since its inception, Bitcoin has been the best-performing financial asset and may be considered to offer an asymmetrical risk profile because its potential for appreciation may be greater than its return to zero. There is speculation that the approval of a spot ETF will accelerate institutional adoption. Ease of access and regulatory transparency of a registered ETF support such speculation, but it is still speculation at this writing.

Artificial Intelligence (AI) for Investors

The advent of widely available generative artificial intelligence applications (AI) in late 2022 will surely expand the information and implementation resources available to average investors at little or no cost. It has driven down the cost of computer coding exponentially which implies a significant expansion of useful applications including those that may help us determine our investment risk tolerance and balance it with our appetite for return with a cogent strategy. AI is a disruptive development, and we should respect its potential in the near term to improve many aspects of our ability to obtain information, organize it efficiently, and harness it for our benefit. Will AI replace human judgment? Only time will tell, but it should provide accessible context and computing power with which we can make more informed judgments. We cannot at this point trust the accuracy of all the output of AI, so must subject it to our own research and judgment.

It is also essential for us to set realistic expectations about our investment programs based on a solid perspective of likely financial behavior. No, AI will not make us all successful stock traders, if for no other reason than ever more sophisticated and faster algorithms used by more powerful entities will allow arbitrage to reduce opportunities for outsized profits. Arbitrage is nothing more than identifying anomalies among prices of generally similar securities that may be caused by minor pricing inefficiencies. The minor pricing inefficiencies narrow and disappear as more arbitrageurs identify the pricing opportunities.

I expect that some firms may begin to offer more sophisticated, portfolio-holding-specific probability modeling that allows individual investors to project returns using the same type of prospect theory that my firm now offers.

Of course, the major firms have economies of scale and can develop customer-facing applications, but it is not always the case that their clients benefit from such economies. They highly likely will not willingly cannibalize their current, very high-profit margin asset management businesses, so it is important for the investor to understand the cost of such services, as highlighted throughout this book.

What is fascinating now is that the cost of developing applications has been declining, which will allow more and faster innovation of useful services. The legacy investment advisory business will have to adapt and improve its service at a much lower cost to the end client. Will the human factor and comfort from such connections be replaced? For many, the answer is no, if only because of inertia and fear of the unknown. But for those who think and act independently, yes. It is probable that some independent investors will not need the continuous supervisory services and their attendant expenses, but as time passes their number will probably increase. It will increase with awareness of viable alternatives and the high cost of doing things the same. Of course, a lower-cost consultative service like the one that I offer will serve the interests of many as well, at least until the fuller development of machine learning and automated advisory systems. Will such services replace human-to-human connection and trust?

IMPLICATIONS OF INDEX TRACKING FOR INSTITUTIONAL FUNDS

The career risk for fund sponsor investment officers is elevated if their fund performed poorly compared to their peer funds due to traveling the less well-worn path represented by strategies of emerging managers. The only way to perform better than the average or median fund is to be unconventional. The trend in institutional performance is that it has tended to be clustered around returns that compare to those generated by a composite of major stock and bond index rates of return in proportion to peer fund asset allocations. As already noted, John Maynard Keynes said: "Worldly wisdom teaches that it is better for the reputation to fail conventionally than to succeed unconventionally."

The tendency for institutional investment programs to produce roughly comparable results for similar types of programs is what I observed over many years of monitoring performance for comparative purposes for my clients. The advent of stock index fund investing removed the reputation risk for decision-makers whose stock performance would always be remarkably close to that of the comparative index against which their program performance may have been evaluated. The added utility of the argument to simply buy a broad index of stocks and save on management fees is significant. Despite the power of the indexing argument, there is a demand for managed portfolios because incremental rates of return compounded, even if only one or two percent a year, are enormous over time. Note that I did not say "passive investing," one can supposedly practice with index investing. Any portfolio decision is an active decision—there is no passivity about investing, as every decision is intentional even if it is to allocate to an index fund. As an aside, the vernacular in the investment industry is often confusing to non-professionals, and I have tried to avoid such terms but define them in plain English.

The professionals at nearly every investment firm that my firm researched were ethical and diligent in their strategy. (I say nearly because we did see some dishonest practitioners, including Madoff, whom we avoided because they could not credibly explain how they managed to produce such returns with only rare monthly declines in value for the five years that ended December 1998, which was ten years before the world learned of the fraud.) The honest practitioners' intention is to produce added value over a relevant measurable index, and all are acutely aware of their responsibility to their respective investors. One could reasonably conclude that investment managers could be deemed to be successful if they perform better than their relevant benchmarks, but also that the industry is subject, if not hostage to *structural mediocrity*. In other words, generating a net of fee performance record that is about in the middle of a peer group is typically good enough to keep the client assets under management and keep the investment manager's job secure.

This brings us to the obvious argument about whether such firms are just asset gatherers or are more focused on client returns. There are many wealthy former investment managers whose firms grew their assets under management but who never produced persistently competitive relative rates of return. That apparent dichotomy is at the core of my message in this book. It is possible, although very difficult to identify consistently competitive investment managers, but worth the effort for marginal allocations to enhance potential performance if one approaches the challenge within a framework of diligent and informed review.

The good news is that one can efficiently and for little cost invest in index funds to participate in the prospects of the financial markets. Marginal allocations to more creative strategies of smaller, perhaps newer firms take much more effort, but if sized appropriately can enhance total portfolio performance. Of course, my firm sought those who could demonstrate structural advantages and other attributes that were compelling for multiple marginal allocations of about 5% of the portfolio. The most important attributes that we sought are humility, passion, and the ability to express their strategy and its advantage with clarity and simplicity. This effort was a full-time process that was labor intensive, because as mentioned earlier, it is the qualitative factors of a strategy that will define its future success. We have all seen the disclaimers that tell us that past performance is not necessarily indicative of future results, so it is important to understand the structural advantages of a strategy and its manager.

What I always brought to the table was an abiding and humble respect for a disciplined and consistent framework for research and portfolio management, and the need to identify a clear structural advantage in any investment strategy that I considered for my clients. I also respect the tendency for behavior and financial markets to return to their average (mean). The financial behavior that is expressed in market performance can inform us about probabilities. It happens that such probability analysis served clients well through significant stock market declines, and while there is no assurance that past patterns will repeat, they are the best we have for assessing the future. As a former Air Force Navigator, I respected the planning process and the requirement to stay on course, which in investing meant staying on a strategy and not panicking due to a stock market decline.

INVESTMENT ADVISOR DUE DILIGENCE CHECKLIST

The Questions Every Investor Should Ask Their Advisor

Markers of future investment success include the following attributes: humility, passion, transparency, and the ability to simply describe the manager's strategy.

Ask yourself these questions first:

- Can you trust the advisor?
- Is the advisor passionate about their process?
- Are the advisor's explanations simply stated?

Clients should ask incumbent or potential investment advisers basic questions:

- How does the advisor add value? How does the advisor measure value add and how frequent are the reports? What documentation can the advisor offer to substantiate its potential to add value?

- Is the advisor independent, or a captive of a larger organization through which it may be required to adhere to the purchase of securities sponsored by the larger organization? If captive, what are the advantages for the client?

- What are the structural advantages of the advisor's investment process?

- What is the advisor's business plan and profile of clients? Where would my account fit into your profile?

- Does the advisor provide contact information for client references upon request?

- Does the advisor provide net of fee performance reports for the most recent interval, usually three months, one year, or more, and since inception compared to relevant, documented returns of peer or individual index and/or composite rates of total return? Does the advisor provide a net of fee and estimated after-tax total rates of return? Can the advisor quantify the advantage of its tax loss harvesting?

- How and when does the advisor receive financial compensation for its services? Will they negotiate fees? Are they fully transparent? Are they exclusively asset-based fees for which the client receives a complete periodic, ideally quarterly report? Does the advisor receive commissions or other compensation related to its client accounts? If so, does the advisor provide detailed reports of such commissions? Does the advisor pay for services with client brokerage commissions or receive a 12(b)1 fee from mutual funds? 12(b)1 fees are levied by mutual funds for marketing expenses and can be paid to advisors using those funds.

- How does the advisor evaluate a client's tolerance for risk of loss and potential for gain? Is the process objective, structured, and fully documented? Does the advisor synthesize a client's investment goals, risk tolerance, and other requirements vital to the client in an investment policy statement? Does the advisor review the client's investment policy statement and risk tolerance at least annually?

- Does the advisor provide relevant educational content and perspective to its clients?

- Does the advisor have any conflicts of interest with the client?

- Be certain to review the advisor's Privacy Policy, SEC Forms, and FINRA reports which should be readily available from the advisor, who should provide URL links to the relevant regulatory documents.

ABOUT THE AUTHOR

ANDREW PARRILLO was an institutional investor for over four decades, the last twenty-five years of which were with his own registered investment advisory firm, Newport Capital Advisers LLC that served endowment funds and family investment offices on a discretionary and non-discretionary basis. The problems that he has solved for former clients and wants to solve with this book are to eliminate the anxiety that individuals may have about investing, to eliminate or greatly reduce their ongoing fees and to produce optimal outcomes with their money. The three questions that investors must answer about investing are: How much risk they want, how much risk they have in their portfolio and how much risk do they need to achieve their goals. He relates what worked for investors over those decades and what he discusses in *Beat the Wealth Management Hustle* is his reality, not a theoretical idea.

He was inspired to share his perspective and advocacy in the book after receiving questions from strangers who have investment advisors about their investment accounts in late 2022 after the financial markets declined by nearly 20%. It was clear from subsequent conversations with friends who have investment advisors that they did not know how much they paid in advisory fees or if and how their advisor added value to their accounts. The fact is that much has changed in the past twenty years to benefit investors, but the wealth management industry has not.

He has three accomplished sons and three grandchildren and enjoys strength training, cooking, a variety of outdoor activities and walking his large black standard poodle, Enzo.

www.ingramcontent.com/pod-product-compliance
Lightning Source LLC
Chambersburg PA
CBHW060931220326
41597CB00020BA/3489